Navigating Federal Travel

A Q&A Roadmap

Navigating Federal Travel

A Q&A Roadmap

Queen E. Cox

MANAGEMENTCONCEPTSPRESS

MANAGEMENTCONCEPTSPRESS
8230 Leesburg Pike, Suite 800
Tysons Corner, VA 22182
(703) 790-9595
Fax: (703) 790-1371
www.managementconcepts.com

Library of Congress Control Number
2012952367

ISBN 978-1-56726-395-4

Printed in the United States of America

10 9 8 7 6 5 4 3 2 1

About the Author

Queen E. ("Queenie") Cox has more than 36 years of military and federal government experience in finance, budgeting, and travel. Prior to retiring in 2008 as Travel & Transportation Management Officer, she held the position of Director, Office of Finance and Budget, at the U.S. International Trade Commission. Her knowledge and experience in financial management and travel enabled her to:

- Identify and implement cost-saving initiatives for travel
- Interpret laws and rules pertaining to the Federal Travel Regulation
- Write travel policies, handbooks, travel alerts, and Q&As
- Provide training on government travel rules and regulations for staff at all levels.

Prior to implementation of the GSA eTravel initiative, she implemented an eTravel system that saved her agency approximately $500,000 in the first four years. Based on that experience, she became a member of the GSA eTravel Team.

Queenie also worked with various GSA interagency workgroups, such as the Agency/Organization Program Coordinators, which assisted GSA in creating *A Guide for Managing Your GSA SmartPay Travel Charge Card Program*. She also served as chairperson of the interagency workgroup that redefined the identifiers/codes for travel that are currently being used government-wide.

Queenie is co-founder of a Washington, D.C., travel-based organization called WO-MEN Travel Professionals (www.wo-men-travelprofessionals.org), which includes both government and industry travel professionals. She has been a contributing columnist for the monthly travel newsletter, the *Federal Travel Report* (published by Management Concepts) since 2009.

Contents

Preface

The Administrator of General Services promulgates the Federal Travel Regulation (FTR) to (1) interpret statutory and other policy requirements in a manner that balances the need to ensure that official government travel is conducted in a responsible manner with the need to minimize administrative costs and (2) communicate the resulting policies clearly to federal agencies and employees. Federal travel is also governed and interpreted by other policy and mandated documents such as executive orders issued by the President of the United States, various circulars, memoranda, and bulletins issued by the Office of Management and Budget (OMB), and legal decisions issued by the Government Accountability Office (GAO) and the Civilian Board of Contract Appeals (CBCA), formerly the General Services Board of Contract Appeals (GSBCA).

This guidebook is based on those policy documents and other mandated documents resulting from congressional action. It is intended to provide government-wide generic guidance for civilian employees who are directed to perform official government travel using appropriated funds. However, it is not a policy handbook. Should there be a conflict between a statement in this guide and the FTR, the FTR takes precedence.

Navigating Federal Travel: A Q&A Roadmap is also intended to serve as a reference for federal employees who are responsible for managing all aspects of government travel. These employees include individuals authorized to approve official government travel using appropriated funds and to determine the need for travel, how the employee is to pay for expenses incurred in performing official travel, and how the employee is to be reimbursed for authorized travel and travel-related expenses. It is also directed to those responsible for managing the government travel charge card program. This guide does not cover every conceivable travel situation; in particular, it does not cover travel related to government aircraft, government ships, or threatened law enforcement and investigative employees. Nor does it cover travel rules for uniformed personnel.

A critical missing component in the management of government travel since the implementation of eTravel has been a dedicated senior position within federal agencies. An agency may have at least one employee assigned to manage its travel program. Even though this responsibility is a major component—and budgeted item—of accomplishing an agency's mission, it is often regarded as an unwelcome "other duties as assigned" task. Unlike other government positions classified by the Office of Personnel Management (OPM), there are no position classification standards for someone who manages government travel. For example, there is no occupational series or position classification for a "travel manager."

Consequently, individuals who manage travel, even for more than 50 percent of their daily duties or responsibilities, do not have the benefit of training that other occupational positions such as a budget analyst, accounting technician, or management analyst are provided. Travel management is learned mainly through on-the-job experience and by sharing best practices with other colleagues who manage government travel.

Managing government travel is a skill; to achieve efficiency and cost savings, a dedicated position is needed. Executive Order (EO) 13589, *Promoting Efficient Spending*, was issued on November 9, 2011, to fill that void in managed government travel. Section 3, Travel, states that "Each agency, agency component, and office of inspector general should designate a senior-level official to be responsible for developing and implementing policies and controls to ensure efficient spending on travel and conference-related activities . . . ." OMB subsequently issued M-12-12, dated May 11, 2012, providing additional guidance to agencies on managing government travel.

The FTR is the "bible" for managing government travel. However, it does not capture every conceivable travel situation or commonsense rule for travel. It therefore falls to legal experts, such as the CBCA and the Comptroller General, to provide interpretation, clarification, or the intended spirit of a law on which the FTR is based. Depending on the implementing legislation, such interpretation or clarification may be required from Congress or OMB.

Navigating Federal Travel consolidates various mandated and implementing travel documents into one document and can thus serve as a handy reference for those who manage government travel. It is formatted in a straightforward and concise question-and-answer format similar to the FTR, with examples of situations that a civilian traveler might encounter before, during, and after approval of authorized travel. It includes specific sections of the FTR and decisions of the GAO and the CBCA (and its predecessor, the GSBCA). In addition, it provides important reference citations that may assist in determining the appropriate method for traveling and resolving travel matters.

Since travel on government-appropriated funds must be authorized and approved in accordance with established travel rules, policies, and regulations, including agency-specific policy, this guidebook should be used as a supplement rather than a replacement for official training on the FTR. Used as a supplement, it is intended to provide a better understanding of the FTR and clarification through cited references and litigated examples.

Although not stated in each instance, travelers should always contact their agency travel manager and other appropriate agency officials, including their agency's ethics officer, human resources manager, and inspector general for further guidance and assistance.

Happy—and productive—trails!

—*Queenie Cox*
September 2012

Acknowledgments

Thanks to the GSA E-Government Travel Program Management Office (now the GSA Center for Travel Management), which had the vision for eTravel. That vision resulted in the consolidation of more than 250 different travel booking, authorization, and financial systems that had not previously incorporated the rules for government travel. It also improved government operations by saving millions of taxpayers' dollars each year as intended by the E-Government Act of 2002. Now on to ETS2 for increased efficiency and savings!

In addition, the eTravel Initiative allowed agency travel managers to focus on managing their agency's travel program, including use of the government travel charge card, more efficiently and effectively. Those travel managers were able to become their agency's subject matter experts on government travel.

And a very special thanks to my friends and former eTravel Team colleagues who became members of WO-MEN Travel Professionals (www.wo-men-travelprofessionals.org). They were willing to share experiences and best practices as a result of eTravel—and continue to do so.

PART I

Terms and Definitions for Purposes of Travel

It is important to understand the myriad terms associated with government temporary duty (TDY) travel. Many travel disputes could be avoided or resolved simply by understanding the terms and how they are used. The following are some of the most common terms that relate to federal travel. For additional terms, consult with your agency travel manager and refer to the current Federal Travel Regulation (FTR).

Approved accommodation

Any place of public lodging that is listed on the national master list of approved accommodations. The national master list of approved accommodations is compiled, periodically updated, and published in the *Federal Register* by the Federal Emergency Management Agency (FEMA). Additionally, the approved accommodation list is available on the U.S. Fire Administration's website, www.usfa.fema.gov/hotel/index.htm.

Automated teller machine (ATM) services

Government contractor–provided ATM services that allow cash withdrawals to be charged to a government contractor–issued charge card.

Common carrier

Private-sector supplier of air, rail, or bus transportation.

Conference

A meeting, retreat, seminar, symposium, or event that involves attendee travel. The term "conference" also applies to training activities that are considered to be conferences under 5 CFR 410.404.

Constructive cost

Calculations that show what the allowable travel costs would have been if the employee had traveled according to the recommended guidelines for official travel. When scheduling travel according to personal preference, rather than the most advantageous arrangement to the government, travelers will be reimbursed for the amount of the constructive cost of travel or the actual cost, whichever is less.

Continental United States (CONUS)

The 48 contiguous states and the District of Columbia.

Contract carriers

U.S.-certificated air carriers that are under contract with the government to furnish federal employees and other persons authorized to travel at government expense with passenger transportation service. These include the General Services Administration (GSA) scheduled airline passenger service between selected U.S. cities/airports and between selected U.S. and international cities/airports at reduced fares.

Dependent

An immediate family member of the employee.

Disability

See Employee with a disability.

Domestic partner

An adult in a domestic partnership with an employee of the same sex.

Domestic partnership

A committed relationship between two adults of the same sex, in which they meet all of the following conditions:

- Are each other's sole domestic partner and intend to remain so indefinitely
- Maintain a common residence and intend to continue to do so (or would maintain a common residence but for an assignment abroad or other employment-related, financial, or similar obstacle)
- Are at least 18 years of age and mentally competent to consent to a contract
- Share responsibility for a significant measure of each other's financial obligations (i.e., there is financial interdependence between the partners; does not exclude partnerships in which one partner stays at home while the other is the primary breadwinner)
- Are not married or joined in a civil union to anyone else
- Are not a domestic partner of anyone else
- Are not related in a way that, if they were of opposite sex, would prohibit legal marriage in the U.S. jurisdiction in which the domestic partnership was formed
- Are willing to certify, if required by the agency, that they understand that willful falsification of any documentation required to establish that an individual is in a domestic partnership may lead to disciplinary action and the recovery of the cost of benefits received related to such falsification, as well as constitute a criminal violation under 18 U.S.C. 1001, and that the method for securing such certification, if required, will be determined by the agency
- Are willing to disclose promptly, if required by the agency, any dissolution or material change in the status of the domestic partnership.

The definition of domestic partnership also requires that the partners share responsibility for a significant measure of each other's financial obligations. This criterion requires only that there be financial interdependence between the partners and does not exclude partnerships in which one partner stays at home while the other is the primary breadwinner.

E-Gov Travel Service (ETS)

The government-contracted, end-to-end travel management service that automates and consolidates the federal travel process in a self-service web-centric environment; covers all aspects of official travel, including travel planning, authorization, reservations, ticketing, expense reimbursement, and travel management reporting.

Employee with a disability – *see also* Special needs

An employee who has a disability and is otherwise generally covered under the Rehabilitation Act of 1973, as amended (29 U.S.C. 701–797b).

"Disability," with respect to an employee, means:

- Having a physical or mental impairment that substantially limits one or more major life activities
- Having a record of such an impairment
- Being regarded as having such an impairment.

The definition does not include an individual who is currently engaging in the illegal use of drugs, when the covered entity acts on the basis of such use.

"Physical or mental impairment" means:

- Any physiological disorder or condition, cosmetic disfigurement, or anatomical loss affecting one or more of the following body systems: neurological, musculoskeletal, special sense organ, respiratory (including speech organs), cardiovascular, reproductive, digestive, genitourinary, hemic and lymphatic, skin, and endocrine

- Any mental or psychological disorder (e.g., mental retardation, organic brain syndrome, emotional or mental illness, specific learning disabilities).

This definition includes, but is not limited to, such diseases and conditions as cerebral palsy, epilepsy, muscular dystrophy, multiple sclerosis, cancer, heart disease, diabetes, mental retardation, emotional illness, and orthopedic, visual, speech and hearing impairments.

"Major life activities" means functions such as caring for oneself, performing manual tasks, walking, seeing, hearing, speaking, breathing, learning, and working.

"Has a record of such an impairment" means the employee has a history of, or has been classified as having, a mental or physical impairment that substantially limits one or more major life activities.

"Is regarded as having such an impairment" means the employee has:

- A physical or mental impairment that does not substantially limit major life activities but the impairment is treated by the agency as constituting such a limitation
- A physical or mental impairment that substantially limits major life activities as a result of the attitudes of others toward such an impairment
- None of the impairments defined under "physical or mental impairment," but is treated by the employing agency as having a substantially limiting impairment.

Employee

For purposes of TDY allowances, an "employee" is:

- An individual employed by an agency, regardless of status or rank
- An individual employed intermittently in government service as an expert or consultant and paid on a daily when-actually-employed (WAE) basis
- An individual serving without pay or at $1 a year (also referred to as "invitational traveler").

Executive agency

For purposes of TDY allowances, includes:

- An executive agency as defined in 5 U.S.C. 105 (except for government-controlled corporations as defined in 31 U.S.C. 9101)
- A military department
- An office, agency, or other establishment in the legislative branch
- The government of the District of Columbia.

The definition does not include:

- A government-controlled corporation
- A member of Congress
- An office or committee of either or both houses of Congress
- An office, agency, or other establishment in the judicial branch.

Foreign air carrier

An air carrier that does not hold a certificate issued by the United States under 49 U.S.C. 41102.

Foreign area – *see also* Non-foreign area

Any area, including the Trust Territories of the Pacific Islands, situated outside both CONUS and the non-foreign areas.

Government contractor–issued individually billed charge card

A government contractor–issued charge card used by authorized individuals to pay for official travel- and transportation-related expenses for which the contractor bills the employee.

Government-furnished automobile

An automobile (or "light truck," as defined in 41 CFR 101-38, including vans and pickup trucks) that meets one of the following conditions:

- Owned by an agency
- Assigned or dispatched to an agency from the GSA Interagency Fleet Management System
- Leased by the government for a period of 60 days or longer from a commercial source.

Government-furnished vehicle

An automobile or aircraft provided by the government.

Government Transportation Request (GTR) (Standard Form 1169)

A government document used to procure common carrier transportation services; obligates the government to pay for transportation services provided.

Immediate family

Any of the following members of the employee's household at the time he/she reports for duty at the new permanent duty station or performs other authorized travel involving family members:

- Spouse.
- Domestic partner.
- Children of the employee, the employee's spouse, or the employee's domestic partner, who are unmarried and under 21 years of age or who, regardless of age, are physically or mentally incapable of self-support. (The term "children" includes natural offspring; stepchildren; adopted children; grandchildren, legal minor wards, or other dependent children who are under legal guardianship of

the employee, the employee's spouse, or the domestic partner; and unborn children born and moved after the employee's effective date of transfer.)

- Dependent parents (including step- and legally adoptive parents) of the employee, the employee's spouse, or the employee's domestic partner.
- Dependent brothers and sisters (including step- and legally adoptive brothers and sisters) of the employee, the employee's spouse, or the employee's domestic partner, who are unmarried and under 21 years of age or who, regardless of age, are physically or mentally incapable of self-support.

Interviewee

An individual who is being considered for employment by an agency. The individual may currently be a government employee.

Invitational travel

Authorized travel of individuals either not employed or employed (under 5 U.S.C. 5703) intermittently in the government service as consultants or experts and paid on a daily when-actually-employed basis and for individuals serving without pay or at $1 a year when they are acting in a capacity that is directly related to, or in connection with, official activities of the government. Travel allowances authorized for such persons are the same as those normally authorized for employees in connection with TDY.

Lodgings-plus per diem system

The method of computing per diem allowances for official travel in which the per diem allowance for each travel day is established on the basis of the actual amount the traveler pays for lodging, plus an allowance for meals and incidental expenses (M&IE), the total of which does not exceed the applicable maximum per diem rate for the location.

Non-foreign area

The states of Alaska and Hawaii; the commonwealths of Puerto Rico, Guam, and the Northern Mariana Islands; and the territories and possessions of the United States (excluding the Trust Territories of the Pacific Islands).

Official station

An area defined by the agency that includes the location where the employee regularly performs his/her duties or an invitational traveler's home or regular place of business. The area may be a mileage radius around a particular point, a geographic boundary, or any other definite domain, provided no part of the area is more than 50 miles from where the employee regularly performs his/her duties or from an invitational traveler's home or regular place of business. If the employee's work involves recurring travel or varies on a recurring basis, the location where the work activities of the employee's position of record are based is considered the regular place of work.

Permanent duty station (PDS) – *see* Official station

Privately owned automobile

A car or light truck (including vans and pickup trucks) that is owned or leased for personal use by an individual.

Privately owned vehicle (POV)

Any vehicle such as an automobile, motorcycle, aircraft, or boat operated by an individual that is not owned or leased by a government agency and is not commercially leased or rented by an employee under a government rental agreement for use in connection with official government business.

Special conveyance

A commercially rented or hired vehicle other than a privately owned vehicle and other than a vehicle owned or under contract to an agency.

Special needs

Physical characteristics of a traveler not necessarily defined as a disability. Such physical characteristics could include the weight or height of the traveler. See also Employee with a disability.

Temporary duty (TDY) location

A place, away from an employee's official station, where the employee is authorized to travel.

Travel authorization/orders

Written permission to travel on official business. There are three basic types of travel authorizations/orders:

- *Unlimited open.* An authorization allowing an employee to travel for any official purpose without further authorization.
- *Limited open.* An authorization allowing an employee to travel on official business without further authorization under certain conditions, such as travel to specific geographic areas for specific purposes, subject to trip cost ceilings, or for specific periods of time.
- *Trip-by-trip.* An authorization allowing an individual or group of individuals to take one or more specific official business trips; must include specific purpose, itinerary, and estimated costs.

Travel claim

A written request, supported by documentation and receipts where applicable, for reimbursement of expenses incurred in the performance of official travel. Also referred to as a "voucher."

Travel Management Service (TMS)

A service for booking a common carrier (e.g., air, rail, and bus confirmations and seat assignments), lodging accommodations, and car rental services; fulfilling (i.e., ticketing) reservations; providing basic management information on those activities; and meeting other requirements as specified in FTR section 301-73.106. A TMS may include a travel management center (TMC), a commercial ticket office (CTO), an electronically available system, other commercial methods of arranging travel, or an in-house system.

United States

The 48 contiguous states, the District of Columbia, and the states and areas defined under the term "non-foreign area." For purposes of travel on U.S. flag air carriers, defined as the 50 states, the District of Columbia, and the territories and possessions of the United States (49 U.S.C. 40102).

Voucher – *see* Travel claim

PART II

Laws, Regulations, and Mandates

It has long been upheld by the Civilian Board of Contract Appeals (CBCA) that it is the traveler's responsibility to know the government travel rules. Relying on others, including supervisors and travel preparers, for clarification or guidance on travel rules does not release the traveler from responsibility for knowing the rules. CBCA 2525-TRAV, *In the Matter of Nicholas Kozauer* (December 20, 2011), serves as an important reminder that federal employees are held solely responsible for any improper costs they incur, even if they were following the advice of an official.

In the case, Dr. Nicholas Kozauer, a medical officer with the Center for Drug Evaluation and Research of the Food and Drug Administration (FDA), Department of Health and Human Services, received approval to attend the Alzheimer's Association International Conference in Paris.

Several months before his trip, Dr. Kozauer asked his agency travel preparer how to book a hotel room for the six-day conference. The travel preparer sent two email responses. First, she advised him to book the room "through the housing reservation office connected with the meeting," noting that "we will do better cost-wise to make reservations through the organization at what looks like a special rate for attendees." The next day, she clarified that the hotel had to be "a meeting-blocked one or that I have to do it through Omega [the FDA's travel management center]." In response to Dr. Kozauer's question about what would happen if he booked the hotel room and then had to cancel it, the travel preparer told him, "I spoke to the management officer, who said not to worry about it. If we have to cancel your hotel reservation and rebook it, we will reimburse you for the [cancellation] fee."

Dr. Kozauer booked a "meeting-blocked" room at the Pullman Paris Montparnasse, charging his government charge card. About a month before the conference, the agency travel preparer informed Dr. Kozauer that she had to make hotel reservations for him through Omega, the FDA's travel management center. She noted that she had tried to have Omega take over Dr. Kozauer's existing reservation, but the electronic travel system determined that the rate was too expensive. The travel preparer booked a room through Omega at another hotel that met the federal per diem rate for Paris.

When Dr. Kozauer tried to cancel his reservation with the Pullman Montparnasse, he was told that he would be charged for his entire five-night stay because the cancellation was after the cutoff date. Ultimately, the hotel lowered the fee to half the cost of the five-night stay, a total of $838.

Dr. Kozauer submitted a claim for reimbursement of the cancellation fee, but despite the agency travel preparer's assurances, the claim was denied. Dr. Kozauer appealed to the CBCA, seeking reimbursement of the cancellation fee.

The CBCA found that the FDA had correctly denied the claim. Under the FTR (section 301-50.3), federal employees must book official travel through either the E-Gov Travel Service (ETS) or the agency's existing travel management system or center. The head of the agency may grant an exception, but only under the following circumstances FTR section 301-50.4):

- Such use would result in an unreasonable burden on mission accomplishment (e.g., emergency travel is involved and the Travel Management Service (TMS) or ETS is not accessible); you are performing invitational travel; or you have special needs or require disability accommodations
- Such use would compromise a national security interest
- Such use might endanger your life (e.g., you are traveling under the federal witness protection program or you are a threatened law enforcement/investigative officer).

The regulation further provides (FTR section 301-50.5) that, where the employee fails to use either the ETS or the agency travel management system—in this case Omega—the employee is responsible for any additional costs, including cancellation fees.

The CBCA noted that there is no authority under statute or regulation for shifting responsibility for such fees to the government. A representative for the FDA, acknowledging that Dr. Kozauer would not have incurred the cancellation fee if not for the advice of the agency's travel preparer, asked the CBCA for additional time to investigate the facts to determine whether it was possible to extend relief to Dr. Kozauer. The agency representative concluded, however, that the circumstances simply did not permit reimbursement.

The CBCA has repeatedly found that federal employees are responsible for any improper fees incurred when they rely on erroneous advice. Even though Dr. Kozauer was acting on the advice of his agency's federal travel preparer, the CBCA concluded that the FDA had acted correctly in rejecting his claim and Dr. Kozauer was responsible for the total $838 cancellation fee.

Several laws, regulations, policies, and rules based on travel policy are incorporated in the FTR; others are stand-alone, and an educated traveler may need to review those documents. Having an understanding of mandated travel policy documents provides both the traveler and travel manager the foundation needed for maximizing the value of travel spending and providing accountability of taxpayers' funds. The following are the key mandated documents that govern federal travel.

Travel and Transportation Reform Act (TTRA) of 1998

Public Law 105-264 mandates that federal employees use the government contractor–issued travel charge card for all payments of expenses related to official government travel unless an exemption has been granted.

Consolidated Appropriations Act of 2006

Section 846 of Public Law 109-115 requires each executive department and agency to evaluate the credit worthiness of an individual before issuing the individual a government travel charge card.

OMB Circular A-123, Appendix B

Often known simply as "Appendix B," OMB Circular A-123 prescribes the policies and procedures agencies must follow to maintain internal controls that reduce the risk of fraud, waste, and error in government charge card programs.

Federal Travel Regulation

41 CFR Parts 300–304 implement statutory requirements and policies for travel by federal civilian employees and others authorized to travel at government expense. Agency policy cannot be less stringent than this regulation.

Fly America Act

49 U.S.C. 40118 requires travelers to use U.S. flag carrier service and service provided under a code-share agreement with a foreign air carrier.

Joint Travel Regulations (JTR)

The governing regulation for federal civilian Department of Defense (DoD) employees. The JTR is guided by the FTR and is based on the same civilian governing statutes, regulations, and policies for civilian travel that are based on the FTR.

Department of State Standardized Regulations for Government Civilians in Foreign Areas

The Secretary of State is responsible for establishing the maximum rates of per diem allowances and reimbursements for the actual and necessary expenses of official travel for employees of the government for travel in foreign areas as authorized by 5 U.S.C. 5702. Foreign per diem rates, which are published in Department of State Standardized Regulations (DSSR), Section 925, are updated monthly and are effective the first day of each month. The rates consist of a maximum lodging portion and a maximum meals and incidental expenses (M&IE) portion. Because taxes are included in the lodging and meal prices used to determine the foreign per diem rates, tax expenses may not be reimbursed separately. The incidental expenses portion of the per diem rate includes laundry and dry cleaning expenses. Therefore, these expenses may not also be claimed separately.

Per diem travel policy, both foreign and domestic, is governed by the FTR and not by the DSSR.

5 U.S.C. Chapter 57

Commonly referred to as Title 5, 5 U.S.C. Chapter 57 prescribes the allowances for travel, transportation, and subsistence as outlined in public laws and also outlines certain agency authorities and responsibilities.

City Pair Program (CPP)

Federal travelers must use the airline City Pair Program (CPP) managed by GSA unless a valid exception applies. GSA manages CPP to provide discounted air transportation services (also known as contract fares) for federal travelers government-wide.

Contract Fares - *see* City Pair Program

Car Rental

Federal travelers should rent vehicles from a vendor that participates in the Defense Travel Management Office (DTMO) U.S. government car rental agreement (unless you are OCONUS and no agreement is in place for your TDY location). Under DTMO, rental car agreements are prenegotiated, unlimited mileage and collision damage insurance are included, and the vendor cannot exceed the rates established.

E-Gov Travel Service (ETS)

Travelers are required to use their agency's ETS and its component units for all travel arrangements unless the agency head or designee grants an exception. An exception is granted only when travel meets one of the following conditions:

- Such use would result in an unreasonable burden on mission accomplishment (e.g., emergency travel is involved and TMS/ETS is not accessible; the traveler is performing invitational travel; the traveler has special needs or requires disability accommodations).
- Such use would compromise a national security interest.
- Such use might endanger the traveler's life (e.g., the individual is traveling under the federal witness protection program or is a threatened law enforcement/investigative officer).
- Any exception granted must be consistent with any contractual terms applicable to the traveler's current TMS or ETS, once it is fully deployed, and must not cause a breach of contract terms.

PART III

The Civilian Board of Contract Appeals

The Civilian Board of Contract Appeals (CBCA) holds the position that travelers are required to know the rules of government travel regardless of their grade or position. This part provides basic information about the CBCA and its legal interpretation of the FTR. Key CBCA decisions provide guidance on specific issues and situations a traveler is likely to encounter.

1 Why was the Civilian Board of Contract Appeals established?

The Civilian Board of Contract Appeals was established by section 847 of the National Defense Authorization Act for Fiscal Year 2006 to hear and decide contract disputes between government contractors and executive agencies under the provisions of the Contract Disputes Act of 1978, 41 U.S.C. 601–613, and regulations and rules issued under that statute.

2 What happened to the General Services Board of Contract Appeals?

On January 6, 2007, the General Services Board of Contract Appeals (GSBCA) ceased to exist, and cases and personnel were transferred to the newly established Civilian Board of Contact Appeals.

3 What types of cases are heard by the CBCA?

The CBCA hears claims by federal employees under 31 U.S.C. 3702 for reimbursement of expenses incurred while on official temporary duty travel or in connection with relocation to a new duty station. In addition, the CBCA hears claims by carriers or freight forwarders under 31 U.S.C. 3726(i)(i) involving actions of the General Services Administration regarding payment for transportation services.

CBCA decisions are available at www.cbca.gov.

4 Can the CBCA review travel reimbursement disputes regarding travel within an official duty station?

Yes. In GSBCA 16083-TRAV, *In the Matter of Carl A. Willecke* (June 11, 2003), the board was presented with an interesting threshold argument by the Army Corps of Engineers. The Corps questioned whether the board's rules of procedure for travel and relocation expenses cases authorized it to review the case. Specifically, the Corps noted that according to the board's rules, it has express jurisdiction over only two types of claims: those for reimbursement of expenses incurred while on official temporary duty travel and those for reimbursement of expenses incurred in connection with relocation to a new duty station.

Since the rules do not expressly grant the board jurisdiction to address claims for local travel, the Corps reasoned that the board lacked the authority to address the issue raised by Willecke in his appeal.

The GSBCA rejected this argument. It found that the Corps had read its rules out of context. The board reminded the Corps that Congress has "vested in the Administrator of General Services the authority to settle claims involving expenses incurred by federal civilian employees for official travel and transportation, and for relocation expenses incident to transfers of official duty station" (31 U.S.C. 3702(a)(3)(2000)).

The FTR, which implements the statutes governing federal civilian employees' travel and relocation, addresses all official travel, including local travel (41 CFR 300-1.1, -1.2, -70.102(h)). Moreover, the JTR, which implements and supplements the FTR for application to Defense Department employees, contains a specific part relating to local travel (JTR C2400-C2404).

Given this statutory and regulatory authority, the GSBCA determined that it clearly has the authority to settle claims for expenses of local travel as well as all other official travel undertaken by federal civilian employees.

5 Who, and what authority, allow an advance decision from the CBCA?

Agency heads and certifying officials have authority to request an advance decision from the CBCA under 31 U.S.C. 3529.

6 What is the Comptroller General's authority compared to the CBCA?

The Comptroller General (CG) has authority under 31 U.S.C. 3529 to issue decisions to disbursing or certifying officers and heads of agencies on matters involving the use of appropriated fund that do not specifically involve settling a claim or other transferred functions as outlined in Public Law 104-316. The CG also has authority under 31 U.S.C. 3527 and 3528 to grant relief to disbursing and certifying officers.

CG decisions are available at www.gao.gov/legal.

PART IV

Before You Travel

In preparation for your official travel, you should become thoroughly familiar with the FTR. Once you have a working understanding of the FTR, you should follow certain steps and be prepared to provide certain information prior to traveling.

This part provides basic information regarding what is required to travel using government funds for official business. When all else fails in determining whether or not a certain expense should be incurred or whether or not a certain type of rental vehicle is considered a luxury car, the federal government has a standard of care for incurring travel expenses that a traveler must follow. This standard of care is also known as "the prudent rule." Simply put, travelers should ask themselves: "If these were my funds, would I . . .?"

> Federal employees and those who are traveling on behalf of the federal government must exercise the same care in incurring expenses that a prudent person would exercise if traveling on personal business.

Another test to determine the appropriateness for traveling or incurring an expense is what is widely known in the Washington, D.C., area as the *Washington Post* test. Simply ask yourself whether or not you or your agency wants to be on the front page of the *Washington Post*. With those two test questions setting the stage for travel, let's look into what you should know before you travel.

7 What is the role of the Administrator of the General Services Administration?

The Administrator of General Services promulgates the FTR to (1) interpret statutory and other policy requirements in a manner that balances the need to ensure that official travel is conducted in a responsible manner with the need to minimize administrative costs and (2) communicate the resulting policies in a clear manner to federal agencies and employees.

8 What is the FTR?

The FTR, contained in Title 41 of the Code of Federal Regulations (CFR), Chapters 300 through 304, implements statutory requirements and executive branch policies for travel by federal civilian employees and others authorized to travel at government expense.

9 What is the purpose of the FTR?

The FTR has two principal purposes:

- To interpret statutory and other policy requirements in a manner that balances the need to ensure that official travel is conducted in a responsible manner with the need to minimize administrative costs
- To communicate the resulting policies in a clear manner to federal agencies and employees.

RESPONSIBILITIES

An important aspect of understanding federal travel is to know the areas of responsibilities. Before a traveler can know what is expected of him/her in performing official travel, the agency must provide certain information. The agency is the first line of defense for ensuring the appropriateness of travel. The approving official is an important enforcer of the agency's written travel policy. Once armed with the required information, the traveler can prepare to perform the official travel as directed.

Agency Responsibilities

Although it appears that a vast majority of the rules in the FTR are discretionary, some rules are mandatory. Travelers and agencies are required to perform certain actions for the traveler to be eligible for reimbursement of travel expenses. Agencies have discretion for authorizing certain travel expenses in a manner that is most effective and efficient for the agency or that is most advantageous to the government. Accordingly, agencies are required to have written established policies based on the various statutes as outlined in 5 U.S.C. Chapter 57. The FTR establishes conditions for payment of travel allowances based on 5 U.S.C. Chapter 57.

10 Why is it important for agencies to have written travel policies?

Having clear written policies makes it easier to determine a traveler's entitlement when compared with any condition noted on the traveler's travel authorization.

> Agency policy cannot be less stringent than or contrary to the FTR.

For example, in GSBCA 15220-TRAV, *In the Matter of Renea A. Webb* (April 10, 2000), an employee of the Inspector General's Office of the Department of Agriculture (USDA) in New Jersey was authorized to travel for training to Maryland. USDA requested that Webb and other employees attending the session who lived in New Jersey carpool to Maryland. The agency informed the employees that if they did not ride together they would receive a reduced mileage rate.

Webb chose to drive alone. After returning, she submitted a travel voucher for mileage expenses based on the POV rate at the time (31 cents per mile). USDA, however, reimbursed her only 23.5 cents per mile. The agency noted that she had been informed that if she chose not to carpool, she would be reimbursed at a reduced mileage rate, citing its Office of Inspector General (OIG) manual as authority for its decision. According to the manual, "all employees traveling by car to the same approximate destination are encouraged to travel in the same vehicle to the maximum extent possible. . . . When an employee chooses not to travel in the authorized vehicle which has been determined as the most advantageous to the government. . .the employee's reimbursement will be subject to a mileage reduction to the least amount allowed by the Federal Travel Regulation (FTR)." At the time of Webb's travel, the minimum mileage rate was 23.5 cents.

Webb appealed to the GSBCA, which determined that she should be reimbursed at the higher rate. The board emphasized that the FTR does not permit an agency to make reimbursement at a lower mileage rate simply because carpooling would be more advantageous to the government than having the employee use his/her own vehicle.

The FTR establishes only two instances where an agency may reimburse an employee at a reduced rate. An agency may limit reimbursement to 23.5 cents per mile if use of a government-furnished car would be more advantageous to the government but a POV is "allowed" nonetheless. Also, agencies may limit reimbursement even further, to 10.5 cents per mile, if an employee is committed to using a government-furnished car or if the employee is not ordinarily authorized to use a POV but still requests to drive his/her own car.

In this case, neither of these exceptions applied. According to the GSBCA, the provision of the OIG manual that allows a reduction in the mileage rate "is plainly at odds with the FTR." Because the FTR was passed by Congress, it overrides any contrary provisions of the agency manual.

11 What specific policies are agencies required to establish for travel?

Agencies must establish policies and procedures governing, at a minimum:

- Who will determine what method of transportation is more advantageous to the government

- Who will approve any of the following:
  - Use of other than coach-class transportation accommodations for air and rail in accordance with the FTR
  - Use of a special reduced fare or reduced group or charter fare
  - Use of an extra-fare train service in accordance with the FTR
  - Use of a foreign air carrier
- When the agency will:
  - Require the use of a government vehicle
  - Allow the use of a government vehicle
  - Prohibit the use of a government vehicle
- When the agency will consider use of a POV advantageous to the government, such as travel to and from common carrier terminals, or transportation to a TDY location
- Procedures for claiming POV reimbursement
- When the agency will allow use of a special conveyance (e.g., commercially rented vehicle)
- What procedures an employee must follow when he/she travels by an indirect route or interrupts travel by a direct route
- Whether to reimburse the full amount of transportation costs in conjunction with TDY or only the amount by which transportation costs exceed the employee's normal costs for transportation between:
  - Office or duty point and another place of business
  - Places of business
  - Residence and place of business other than office or duty point.

Agencies must also:

- develop and issue internal guidance on what specific mission criteria justify approval of the use of other than coach-class transportation in accordance with FTR (with justification criteria entered in the remarks section of the traveler's travel authorization)
- Develop and publish internal guidance regarding what constitutes a rest period upon arrival at a temporary duty location
- Develop and publish internal guidance regarding seating upgrade programs in coach class.

12 May agency policy provide an allowance or entitlement more favorable to the traveler that is less stringent than the FTR?

No. Agencies have the discretion to make their own policies more stringent—but not less stringent—than the FTR. For example, although FTR section 301-11.31 states in part that dry cleaning expenses are reimbursable if the traveler spends a minimum of four consecutive nights lodging on official travel, agency policy might require a minimum of six consecutive nights, which would supersede the FTR policy.

Traveler Responsibilities

Travelers are responsible for preparing and submitting all travel documents, including initial authorizations, amendments, and post-trip vouchers. The traveler is also liable for any false or fraudulent written or oral statements under the False Claims Act (18 U.S.C. 287, 18 U.S.C. 1001 and 31 U.S.C. 3729).

13 What are the traveler's responsibilities?

Overall, travelers are responsible for:

- Being familiar with government travel policies, regulations, and procedures for traveling on government funds
- Performing all official travel within the guidance and direction provided by those policies
- Requesting clarification on the policy of any travel policy, regulation, or procedure that he/she does not understand
- Exercising the standard of care rule when incurring reimbursable travel expenses in the performance of official travel
- Using the mode of transportation that results in the greatest overall advantage to the government
- Planning travel to minimize per diem expense
- Not delaying the performance of official travel for personal benefit

- Paying any additional expenses resulting from scheduling travel for personal convenience and charging excess travel time against leave
- Accounting for funds advanced for travel purposes since the traveler is indebted to the government for those funds
- Using the individually billed travel charge card issued for official travel. (See also *Part V* of this guide, *While on Travel*, regarding paying for your travel expenses with a contractor-issued government travel charge card.)

Approving Official Responsibilities

An approving official for travel must know and understand the regulations and policies that govern the performance of his/her duties. An approving official is required to have written authority delegated by the agency head to determine when TDY travel is necessary to accomplish the agency's mission, authorize travel, obligate travel funds, approve trip arrangements, and authorize travel expenses incurred in connection with that mission.

An approving official must consider the total cost to the government (including costs of per diem, overtime, lost work time, and actual transportation), total distance traveled, number of points visited, number of travelers, and energy conservation. Moreover, an approving official must have full knowledge of the employee's activities.

While reviewing and approving a voucher, the approving official must ensure that:

- The claim is properly prepared in accordance with the pertinent regulations and agency procedures
- A copy of the authorization for travel is provided
- The types of expenses claimed are authorized and allowable expenses
- The amounts claimed are accurate
- The required receipts, statements, justifications, etc., are attached to the travel claim.

The approving official reviews the completed claim to ensure that the claim is properly prepared in accordance with regulations and agency procedures prior to authorization for payment.

An approving official may disallow a claim by a traveler and must provide the reason for the disallowance in writing in accordance with FTR sections 301-52.8 and 301-52.9.

14 When authorizing travel, what factors must the authorizing official consider?

The authorizing official must consider:

- The need for the travel
- The use of travel substitutes (e.g., mail, teleconferencing, videoconferencing)
- The most cost-effective routing and means of accomplishing travel
- The employee's travel plans, including plans to take leave in conjunction with travel.

Additional guidance on authorizing travel is provided in OMB Memorandum M-12-12, *Promoting Efficient Spending to Support Agency Operations* (May 11, 2012) and Executive Order 13589, *Promoting Efficient Spending* (November 9, 2011).

15 What key questions should an approving official consider when authorizing travel?

The approving official should consider these basic questions when authorizing travel:

- Is the travel necessary?
- Are the travel times reasonable?
- Are the total costs correct?
- Are funds available?
- Is the traveler using a contract carrier? If not, does the traveler meet one of the approved exceptions?

- Is a rental car required or needed? Is the size of the car adequate to fulfill the travel mission?
- Are exceptions to policy adequately justified, documented, and authorized?

TRAVEL PREPARATION

When planning and preparing for official government travel, a traveler must comply with the laws, regulations, and mandates regarding:

- When a travel authorization is required
- Preparation of the travel authorization
- Which travel arrangements require specific authorization or advance approval
- When a travel authorization requires an amendment
- Why government travelers are required to use contract fares and the exceptions for not using contract fares
- Defining travel status and when a traveler is entitled to per diem
- Complying with the rules for invitational travel
- Understanding when it is necessary to accommodate a special need.

Travel Authorization

After you receive verbal approval to travel, you are required to prepare a travel authorization (or order) in accordance with FTR section 301-50.3. A travel authorization is a written document that provides permission to travel on official business. The travel authorization notes any condition or allowable expense that is not clearly identified as a part of official travel but does not entitle the traveler to an expense that is illegal or is not authorized under any mandated travel document.

16 What is the purpose of the travel authorization process?

The purpose of the travel authorization process is to:

- Provide the employee information regarding what expenses the agency will pay

- Provide financial information necessary for budgetary planning
- Identify the purpose of travel
- Ensure the travel is approved before it is performed.

17 What are the basic types of travel authorizations allowable for travel?

The basic types of travel authorizations are:

- *Unlimited open* – An authorization that allows an employee to travel for any official purpose without further authorization.
- *Limited open* – An authorization that allows an employee to travel on official business without further authorization under certain specific conditions (such as travel to specific geographic areas for specific purposes, travel subject to trip cost ceilings, or travel for specific periods of time).
- *Trip-by-trip* – An authorization that allows an individual or group of individuals to take one or more specific official business trips, which must include specific purpose, itinerary, and estimated costs. This type of travel authorization is the one most often used by civilian travelers.

18 What information is required on a travel authorization?

A travel authorization must include:

- Name of the employee
- Signature of the proper authorizing official
- Purpose of travel
- Any conditions of or limitations on the authorization
- Estimate of the travel costs (unlimited and limited open authorizations should include an estimate of the travel costs over the period covered)
- Statement that the employee is authorized to travel.

19 What types of conditions or limitations may be stated on a travel authorization?

Many conditions or limitations may be imposed on travel using government funds. These may include: a statement that the traveler is not a government travel charge cardholder; whether or not the traveler is exempt from the mandatory use of a government travel charge card; how the traveler can obtain an advance; whether or not a rest stop is authorized; and specific approval to use a rental car.

20 Why does a traveler need written authorization to travel? Isn't the word of a supervisor good enough?

Although a supervisor may verbally direct a traveler to travel, generally, you must have written or electronic authorization prior to incurring any travel expense. Written or electronic authorization determines travel entitlements and any condition for traveling. You will also need the written or electronic authorization for reimbursement of any travel expense. If it is impossible or impractical to obtain a travel authorization prior to travel, your agency may approve a specific authorization for reimbursement of travel expenses after the travel is completed.

21 Who and what determine a traveler's mode of transportation for travel?

The traveler is entitled to transportation costs to and from the TDY location. The traveler must travel to the destination by the usually traveled route unless the agency authorizes/approves a different route.

Under 5 U.S.C. 5733, travel must be by the most expeditious means of transportation practicable and commensurate with the nature and purpose of the traveler's duties. The agency head is required to have written, established policies and procedures regarding who will determine what method of transportation is more advantageous to the government.

22 What travel arrangements require specific authorization or prior approval?

A government traveler must have a specific authorization or prior approval for:

- Use of other than coach-class service on common carrier transportation.
- Use of a foreign air carrier.
- Use of reduced fares for group or charter arrangements.
- Use of cash to pay for common carrier transportation.
- Use of extra-fare train service.
- Travel by ship.
- Use of a rental car.
- Use of a government aircraft.
- Payment of a reduced per diem rate.
- Payment of actual expense, unless your agency has issued a blanket actual expense authorization for TDY travel in an area subject to a presidentially declared disaster. This authorization must apply to a specific declaration and must end on the expiration date of the declaration or one year from the date the declaration is issued, whichever is sooner. (A blanket authorization issued under this condition does not apply to any travel performed pursuant to relocation allowances.)
- Travel expenses related to emergency travel.
- Transportation expenses (i.e., of things, including animals and household goods) related to threatened law enforcement/investigative employees and members of their families.
- Travel expenses related to travel to a foreign area.
- Acceptance of payment from a nonfederal source for travel expenses.
- Travel expenses related to attendance at a conference.
- Payment of the full M&IE allowance even though meals are furnished by the government either directly or through a registration

fee or other payment for a conference or other event to accommodate an employee's medical requirements or religious beliefs.

> A travel authorization may be amended to correct or complete a travel authorization to show the original intent.

23 If a traveler returns from a trip a day early, does he/she need to amend the authorization to reflect the date change? Conversely, if the trip is extended for official business, does the authorization have to be amended to reflect the changed dates before approving the voucher?

Yes. A traveler must be in a travel status to be paid travel entitlements. Because certain changes to an itinerary that may result in a traveler not being in a travel status or not entitled to an allowance, an amendment is required. Similarly, if a traveler extends a trip for official business, the agency must pay the traveler an allowance; therefore, an amendment is required. Overall, an amendment is required for any condition not previously authorized, such as departing earlier from the TDY station, extending the trip, changing the mode of travel, or in general any change that affects the cost of the trip.

> A travel authorization may not be revoked or modified retroactively to create or deny an allowance.

Passports/Visas

Before traveling overseas to perform official government business, a traveler must have an official passport and, in some cases, a visa. The traveler may also need country clearance before entering a foreign country. The government will generally reimburse the traveler for some of the expenses associated with obtaining an official passport or visa.

24 Can a traveler use a personal passport for official government travel?

No. A traveler must have an official or a diplomatic passport when conducting official government business in a foreign country.

25 Can a traveler be reimbursed for passport and visa fees?

Yes. A traveler may be reimbursed under the miscellaneous expense category for passport and visa fees. This include fees for a physical examination if one is required to obtain a passport or visa and such examination could not be obtained at a government facility.

26 Who determines whether or not a traveler is exempt from the fee for an official passport?

In accordance with the State Department's requirements for processing a no-fee passport, a traveler is exempt by law from payment for the passport if he/she is (1) an officer or employee of the U.S. government traveling abroad for the U.S. government or (2) the dependent of someone traveling abroad for the U.S. government and will accompany them on their assignment.

No-fee passports are issued only in book form. If you are applying for a no-fee passport book at a passport acceptance facility, you will be charged the $25.00 passport execution fee; however, you are not required to pay the passport fee.

27 What other passport and visa fees are reimbursable?

A traveler may also be reimbursed for the costs of photographs for passports and visas; foreign country exit fees; costs of birth, health, and identity certificates; and charges for inoculations that cannot be obtained through a federal dispensary.

28 How can a traveler obtain health information for the country he/she will be traveling to?

Health information regarding travel outside the United States may be obtained from the Centers for Disease Control. Here's the link for information by specific country: http://wwwnc.cdc.gov/travel/destinations/list.htm.

29 Can a traveler be reimbursed for transportation costs incurred while obtaining an official passport or visa?

A traveler may be reimbursed for travel and transportation costs to the passport/visa issuing office if it is located outside the local commuting area of the employee's official station and the traveler's presence at that office is mandatory.

30 Can an official passport be used for personal travel?

No. You may use your no-fee passport book only when traveling overseas while performing official government duties. For personal travel, you must use a regular-fee passport book or card. You may have both a valid regular passport book and a valid no-fee passport book at the same time.

31 Can a traveler pick up an official passport from the passport facility?

Generally, no-fee passport books are sent to or picked up by the organization, government agency, or branch of service sponsoring the passport issuance, not the individual. The sponsor of your official travel should appear in the "mailing address" block of the application.

32 For how long must a passport for official travel be valid?

Your official or diplomatic passport must be valid for at least three months after the travel departure date.

33 When is host country clearance required?

Formal host country clearance is required by most foreign countries for U.S. federal, state, or local officials to conduct judicial assistance activities abroad. This includes taking depositions, interviews, inspections, etc.

34 What is host country clearance?

Sometimes overseas travel requires a country clearance. Prior to the arrival of a U.S official intending to conduct judicial assistance activity abroad, it may be necessary for the U.S. consulate to deliver a diplomatic note to the Ministry of Foreign Affairs. The note explains the purpose of the travel and requests permission for the U.S. official to conduct judicial assistance activity. This notification may or may not be required, depending on the nature and purpose of the trip and the sensitivities of the host country.

35 What will happen if a traveler does not get host country clearance?

Travel without prior clearance can result in arrest, detention, expulsion, or deportation of the official. It can also negatively affect U.S. policy interests and future attempts to gain host country judicial assistance.

36 Is U.S. embassy clearance also required?

Federal executive branch government officials traveling abroad for judicial assistance purposes also require clearance from the U.S. embassy or consulate in the particular country. This requirement is derived from the country authority of ambassadors and chiefs of mission, 22 U.S.C. 3927 and E.O. 10893, Part II, 11/8/60.

37 Can U.S. embassy clearance for travel be denied?

If the proposed official travel coincides with the arrival of a presidential, vice presidential, or congressional delegation, summit meeting, or similar workload-intensive event, it is possible that the embassy will not have the staff or space to support the proposed judicial assistance travel on the proposed date. During time of an international crisis, resulting in the authorized or ordered departure of official personnel from the embassy or consulate or closure of the embassy or consulate, embassy clearance may be denied.

38 Can the embassy or consulate provide interpreters, stenographers, video equipment, etc.?

These services are not available at the embassy or consulate. However, for official travelers involved in judicial assistance matters, embassies and consulates can assist in either retaining foreign host country commercial services (charging them against your federal fiscal data and appropriation number or credit card) or furnish you with information regarding how you can retain such services directly. If no such services are available in the host country, it may be necessary to bring your own support staff. Foreign embassies or consulates in the United States can advise on any special requirements associated with importing electronic equipment to ensure that your equipment is not confiscated.

39 How do I report a lost or stolen passport?

If your passport is lost or stolen while overseas, contact the nearest U.S. embassy or consulate. For more information about a lost or stolen passport, or what to do if you find someone else's passport, call the State Department at 877-487-2778 or visit its website, http://travel.state.gov/passport/lost/lost_848.html.

40 What should a traveler do in the event of unanticipated civil disturbance or unrest while on official travel?

Travelers are encouraged to stay abreast of such matters pertaining to the specific country that will be visited through postings and notifications of travel alerts issued by the State Department. The

State Department's Office of American Citizens Services and Crisis Management administers the Consular Information Program, which informs the public of conditions abroad that may affect their safety and security. Country-specific information, travel alerts, and travel warnings are vital parts of this program; information is available at http://travel.state.gov/travel/travel_1744.html.

41 Can an agency pay the transportation expenses of an employee's dependents during an evacuation?

5 U.S.C. 5725 authorizes the government to pay the transportation expenses of the dependents of a government employee, as well as the expenses incurred in transporting household goods from a foreign location to a safe haven location within the continental United States, when an evacuation is ordered or authorized.

This entitlement is implemented by Chapter 600 of the Department of State Standardized Regulations (DSSR).

42 How can an agency track its overseas travelers in the event of civil unrest?

For an agency to support its overseas travelers, it must first know when and where they are going. The agency can then assist travelers in preparing for the trip in terms of travel documentation, health and immunizations, safety, security, transportation, etc. Using a traveler's itinerary, the agency can quickly identify any impacts of worldwide events, such as catastrophic weather, earthquakes, civil unrest, strikes, etc. The itinerary provides a good starting point for locating a traveler. Various mobile tracking solutions are also available if the agency needs more detailed information.

43 How can an agency integrate travel risk management with ETS to mitigate certain travel risks an international traveler may encounter?

There is currently only one company on the GSA schedule, under the special item number (SIN) 599-1, that provides travel security risk assessment and related training to support travel risk management needs, including travel security needs for international government travelers. That company, iJET International, Inc., uses a risk management system that seamlessly interfaces with the government's etravel initiatives and ETS by linking directly to source itinerary information and thereby providing automated itinerary tracking.

Travel Advance

A travel advance is a prepayment of estimated travel expenses to an employee in advance of travel. A travel advance minimizes an employee's out-of-pocket expenses related to official travel.

44 For what expenses may a traveler receive a travel advance?

A traveler may receive an advance for the following expenses:

For	You may receive an advance
Cash transaction expenses (i.e., expenses that as a general rule cannot be charged and must be paid using cash, a personal check, or traveler's check). These include: ◆ M&IE covered by the per diem allowance or actual expenses allowance ◆ Miscellaneous transportation expenses such as transit system and taxi fares; parking fees; ferry fees; bridge, road, and tunnel fees ◆ Gasoline and other variable expenses covered by the mileage allowance for advantageous use of a privately owned automobile for official business ◆ Other authorized miscellaneous expenses that cannot be charged using a government contractor–issued charge card and for which a cost can be estimated.	Any time you are on official travel.

Non-cash transaction expenses, such as lodging, common carrier, and advance payment of a discounted conference registration fee.	Only in the following situations: ◆ Government contractor-issued charge card is not expected to be accepted. ◆ Government contractor-issued charge card issuance is denied. Your agency has decided not to provide you a government contractor–issued individually billed travel card. ◆ Official change of station. Your agency determines that use of a government contractor–issued individually billed travel card would not be feasible incident to a transfer, particularly a transfer to another agency. ◆ Financial hardship would be incurred.

45 What is the maximum amount that an agency may advance?

The amount your agency advances may not exceed the following amounts:

For	The maximum amount your agency may advance is
Cash transaction expenses	The estimated amount of your cash transaction expenses. (For M&IE, your advance is limited to the M&IE rate under the lodgings-plus per diem method.)
Non-cash transaction expenses	Generally zero. However, your agency may advance up to the full amount of your expected non-cash transaction expenses for an individual trip (not to exceed a 45-day period for an open authorization) in accordance with the FTR.

46 When must a traveler account for an advance?

A traveler must file a travel claim that accounts for the advance after completion of the travel, in accordance with agency policy. If a traveler is in a continuous travel status (e.g., an auditor or inspector) or if the traveler submits periodic reimbursement vouchers on an individual trip authorization, the agency may reimburse the traveler the full amount of travel expenses without any deduction of the advance until the traveler files a final voucher. If the amount advanced is less than the amount of the voucher on which it is deducted, the traveler will be reimbursed the net amount. If the advance exceeds the reimbursable amount, the traveler must refund the excess immediately.

47 What is general agency policy governing the use of travel advances?

Agencies should minimize the use of cash travel advances. However, an agency should not require an employee to pay travel expenses using personal funds unless the employee has elected not to use alternative resources provided by the government, such as a government contractor–issued charge card.

48 In situations where a lodging facility requires the payment of a deposit, may an agency reimburse an employee for an advance room deposit prior to the beginning of scheduled official travel?

Yes. When an advance room deposit is required by the lodging facility to secure a room reservation, the agency may reimburse an employee the deposit prior to the beginning of the employee's scheduled official travel. However, if the employee is reimbursed the advance room deposit but fails to perform the scheduled official travel for reasons not acceptable to the agency, resulting in forfeit of the deposit, the employee is indebted to the government and must repay the amount in a timely manner as prescribed by the agency.

49 For how long may an agency issue a travel advance?

The agency may issue a travel advance for a reasonable period not to exceed 45 days.

50 What data must an agency capture in its travel advance accounting system?

An agency must capture the following data in its travel advance accounting system:

- The name and Social Security number of each employee who has has received an advance
- The amount of the advance
- The date of issuance
- The date of reconciliation for unused portions of travel advances.

51 When must an employee account for a travel advance?

An employee must account for an outstanding travel advance each time he/she files a travel claim. If the employee receives a travel advance but determines that the related travel will not be performed, then the employee must inform the agency that the travel will not be performed and repay the advance at that time.

52 May travelers be reimbursed for stolen travel advances?

No. An advance of funds is considered a personal loan to the traveler. If the funds were in the custody of the traveler, the traveler is responsible and accountable for the funds. The government must recoup the funds if the traveler cannot show that the funds were spent for official travel-related expenses or returned. The government is not obligated to relieve the employee from liability to repay stolen funds; however, under the agency's policy, it has discretion to resolve the claim under 31 U.S.C. 3721.

For example, in GSBCA 13872-TRAV, *In the Matter of William O'Callaghan* (May 16, 1997), an employee of the U.S. Agency for International Development (USAID) was authorized for TDY in the Ukraine. Because traveler's checks and credit cards are not generally accepted in the Ukraine, O'Callaghan requested and was granted a cash advance of $3,000 for meals, lodgings, and incidental expenses.

Upon arriving in the Ukraine, he was advised by the local USAID office that he should not leave cash or valuables in his hotel due to the threat of theft. Accordingly, O'Callaghan carried his cash and valuables on his person.

Unfortunately, he was attacked and robbed after leaving a colleague's birthday party, which had been held in O'Callaghan's hotel. Although the robbery did not take place during working hours, O'Callaghan and other attendees worked part of the time by placing phone calls to USAID headquarters in Washington, D.C., and discussing business-related issues.

The assailant absconded with most of O'Callaghan's travel advance and several personal items, and O'Callaghan was hospitalized for nine hours after the attack. He filed a claim under the Military Personnel and Civilian Employees' Claim Act. USAID denied the claim on the basis that the loss did not occur during official working hours or on official premises. The fact that he made a few phone calls and spoke with attendees about business matters did not turn the party into an official event for which the agency was responsible.

O'Callaghan appealed to the GSBCA. USAID argued that O'Callaghan was precluded from raising the claim with the board. The agency emphasized that the Personnel and Civilian Employees' Claim Act provided the sole remedy for O'Callaghan, and he had exhausted that remedy when it denied his claim.

The board agreed with USAID's argument. It noted that GAO had ruled previously that travel advances are personal loans for which the government is not obligated to relieve employees from liability for stolen amounts. In addition, the FTR authorizes only the reimbursement of travel expenses essential to the transaction of official business.

O'Callaghan's loss of personal belongings was therefore not considered a reimbursable expense under the FTR.

53 Are there exceptions to the agency's collecting an advance at the time the employee files a travel claim?

Yes, when the employee is in a continuous travel status such as an auditor or inpector and the agency:

- Reviews each outstanding travel advance on a periodic basis (i.e., a reasonable time of 45 days or less)
- Determines that the amount, if any, of the outstanding balance exceeds the amount of estimated travel expenses for the authorized period and collects the excess amount from the employee.

54 Is the agency responsible for collecting outstanding travel advances? How does the agency collect the amount of a travel advance that exceeds the amount of the travel expenses substantiated by the employee?

Yes, the agency is responsible for collecting outstanding travel advances. When the outstanding advance exceeds the amount the agency owes the employee, then the employee must submit cash or a check for the difference in accordance with agency policy. If the agency fails to collect the amount that is in excess of substantiated expenses, it will be in violation of the accountable plan rules contained in the Internal Revenue Code (title 26 of the United States Code).

55 What should an agency do if the employee does not pay back a travel advance when the travel claim is filed?

If the employee fails to pay back a travel advance when the claim is filed, the agency should take steps to collect the debt, for example:

- Offset the amount against the employee's salary, retirement credit, or other amount owed the employee
- Deduct the amount from another amount the government owes the employee
- Pursue any other legal method of recovery.

56 What internal policies and procedures must an agency establish governing travel advances?

Accountability for cash advances for travel, recovery, and reimbursement must be in accordance with procedures prescribed by GAO (see the *GAO Policy and Procedures Manual for Guidance of Federal Agencies, Title 7, Fiscal Procedures – Transmittal Sheet No.7-43 dated May 18, 1993*).

Contract Fares

Travelers are required to use the GSA City Pair Program (CPP), which offers contract fares unless a specific exception applies for official travel.

57 Why are government travelers required to use contract fares when cheaper fares may be available on the internet?

Extensive analysis shows that the flexibility of contract fares provides government travelers the best deal overall, compared to volatile commercial airline rates.

CPP features allow government travelers unsurpassed flexibility. Fares are unrestricted, meaning that:

- No advance purchase is required
- No minimum or maximum length of stay is required
- Tickets are fully refundable
- There is no fee for cancellations or changes
- Last seat availability
- There are no blackout periods.

58 What does last seat availability mean?

Last seat availability means that if any economy seats are available for purchase, government travelers will be guaranteed the CPP standard fare. Last seat availability refers to a price guarantee and not where a traveler sits on the plane. Last seat availability does not include seat assignment preference.

59 What is a capacity control fare and how does it differ from a YCA fare?

There are two contract fares, also known as dual fares. The most commonly known and used fare is a YCA fare, which is a highly discounted, unrestricted fare. A capacity control fare is a fare that has a deeper discount than a YCA fare if the traveler can book early and the fare is identified as a dash CA (_CA) fare.

If travel plans are certain (e.g., attending a conference or training) or the traveler's schedule is flexible, a _CA fare offers additional savings. The price differential between YCA and _CA fares varies by market, but can be significant.

The earlier the reservation is made, the greater the chances that an agency will receive the additional savings that _CA fares offer. With a _CA fare, the traveler enjoys all the benefits of an unrestricted YCA fare.

60 Under what circumstances can non-contract fares be used?

An agency may authorize use of a fare other than a contract city-pair fare in the following situations:

- Space on a scheduled contract flight is not available in time to accomplish the purpose of the travel, or the use of contract service would require the traveler to incur unnecessary overnight lodging costs, increasing the total cost of the trip.
- The contractor's flight schedule is inconsistent with the explicit policies of the traveler's federal department or agency with regard to scheduling travel during normal working hours.
- A non-contract carrier offers a lower fare to the general public that will result in a lower total trip cost to the government (considering the combined costs of transportation, lodging, meals, and related expenses). This exception does not apply if the contract carrier offers the same or lower fare and has seats available at that fare, or if the fare offered by the non-contract carrier is restricted to government and military travelers performing official business. The non-contract fare may be purchased only with a contractor-issued charge card, centrally billed account, or GTR (when the two previous options are not available).
- Cost-effective rail service is available and is consistent with mission requirements.

- Smoking is permitted on the contract air carrier and the nonsmoking section of the contract aircraft is not acceptable to the traveler.

61 Can a contract fare be used for personal travel?

No. The use of contract fares is limited to official travel only. If personal travel is being taken in conjunction with official government travel, the contract fares cannot be used for the portion of the trip that is personal. The traveler is required to purchase the personal portion of the trip separately from the official government travel. No personal stops should be reflected on the official travel itinerary.

The agency may also collect from travelers the cost of any airfare purchased for them if the travelers exchange the tickets for non-refundable fares that include personal travel and the agency subsequently cancels the official tickets. For example, in GSBCA 14051-TRAV, *In the Matter of Judy Van Alfen* (November 7, 1997), an employee of the Internal Revenue Service (IRS) in Washington, D.C., was authorized to travel to Cincinnati, Ohio. The agency approved air travel for the trip and purchased a ticket on a government contract carrier for her in the amount of $408.

Van Alfen decided that she wanted to combine some personal travel with her trip to Ohio, so she exchanged the ticket purchased by her agency for one that included personal travel. The new ticket was non-refundable.

Shortly before her departure date, the IRS canceled her trip due to other pressing business and requested that she refund the $408 spent on her original ticket. Van Alfen refused. She argued that the new ticket was non-refundable. Moreover, the ticket was forfeited as a result of the agency's decision to cancel her trip.

Van Alfen appealed to the General Services Board of Contract Appeals (GSBCA), but the board rejected her appeal. It emphasized that the FTR is clear that if, for personal convenience, an employee elects to modify arrangements made for official travel, he/she is responsible for any resulting additional cost.

If Van Alfen had not exchanged the original ticket for a non-refundable one that included personal travel, the government would have received a refund for canceling her trip. Therefore, the amount of the original ticket represented the cost Van Alfen must pay for modifying her travel arrangements.

62 Can personal travel be combined with official travel?

Yes, personal travel may be combined with official travel. However, the traveler is responsible for any additional charges resulting from the personal travel, including traveling by an indirect route or extending an official stopover for more than four hours.

The traveler may not use the government travel charge card for personal travel, or use government contract fares for any personal leg of the trip or to calculate a difference in fares for personal travel. Also, the traveler's official itinerary should not reflect personal stops or paid per diem while in a leave status.

To ensure compliance with the FTR, the official travel should be ticketed and issued separately from the personal travel. The traveler may then exchange the ticket with the official itinerary for a new one to accommodate the personal travel, and pay any additional fees at that time.

Per Diem

Per diem allowance (also referred to as subsistence allowance) is a daily payment instead of reimbursement for actual expenses for lodging, meals, and related incidental expenses. The per diem allowance is separate from transportation expenses and other miscellaneous expenses. The per diem allowance covers all charges, including any service charges where applicable. Lodging taxes in the United States are excluded from the per diem allowance and are reimbursed as a miscellaneous expense. In foreign locations, lodging taxes are part of the per diem allowance and cannot be separated or reimbursed as a miscellaneous expense.

63 Does GSA establish all per diem rates?

No. The General Services Administration (GSA) establishes per diem rates in the continental United States (CONUS). For travelers to

CONUS locations, laundry, dry cleaning, and taxes on lodging may be reimbursed in addition to the per diem rate.

The Department of Defense establishes per diem rates for non-foreign locations outside the continental United States, such as Alaska, Hawaii, or Guam. Travelers to these non-foreign "OCONUS" locations may claim lodging tax expenses separately, but may not claim laundry and dry cleaning expenses as those expenses are included in the incidental expenses portion of the OCONUS per diem rate, as stated in FTR section 301-11.31.

Foreign per diem rates are established by the Secretary of State for reimbursement of government civilians traveling on official business in foreign areas. Lodging and M&IE (meals and incidental expenses) are reported separately followed by a combined daily rate. The M&IE portion is intended to substantially cover the cost of meals and incidental travel expenses such as laundry and dry cleaning. Therefore, laundry and dry cleaning may not be claimed separately or as a miscellaneous expense for foreign travel.

64 What policies is an agency required to establish for authorization and payment of per diem expenses?

Agencies must establish policies and procedures governing:

- Who will authorize a rest period
- Circumstances allowing a rest period during prolonged travel
- Whether, and in what instances, an employee is allowed to return to his/her official station on non-workdays
- Who will determine whether an employee will be allowed to return to his/her official station on a case-by-case basis
- Who will determine in what instances a reduced per diem rate will be paid
- Who will determine, and in what instances, whether a blanket authorization will be issued for actual expenses in accordance with the FTR or when actual expenses are appropriate in individual cases
- Who will determine, and in what instances, whether an employee will be able to claim the full M&IE allowance even though meals

are furnished to the employee by the government, in accordance with the FTR.

65 What does the per diem allowance cover?

The per diem allowance covers:

- *Lodging*- Expenses except lodging taxes in the United States, for overnight sleeping facilities, baths, personal use of the room during daytime, telephone access fee, and service charges for fans, air conditioners, and heaters furnished in the room when such charges are not included in the room rate.
- *Meals*- Expenses for breakfast, lunch, dinner, and related tips and taxes. (Specifically excluded are alcoholic beverage and entertainment expenses, and any expenses incurred for other persons.)
- *Incidental expenses*:
  - Fees and tips given to porters, baggage carriers, hotel staff, and staff on ships
  - Transportation between places of lodging or business and places where meals are taken, if suitable meals cannot be obtained at the TDY site
  - Mailing costs associated with filing travel vouchers and payment of government-sponsored charge card billings.

66 What is a standard CONUS location?

A standard CONUS location is a location that is less frequently traveled by the federal community and therefore is not specifically listed with the non-standard CONUS per diem rates. If neither the city nor the county is listed on the per diem listing, it is considered a standard CONUS designation.

67 When is a traveler eligible for per diem or travel allowances?

A traveler is eligible for per diem or travel allowances when three conditions are met:

- The employee performs official travel away from his/her official station, or other areas defined by the agency.
- The employee incurs an authorized expense while performing official travel.
- The employee is in a travel status for more than 12 hours.

68 For purposes of per diem, when does TDY travel begin and end?

Travel begins when the traveler departs from home, office, or any other authorized point and ends when the traveler returns to that point (FTR section 301-11.9).

In CBCA 2249-TRAV, *In the Matter of Roger Chalonec* (March 2, 2011), an employee of the Pension Benefit Guaranty Corporation traveled round-trip from his home in Port Tobacco, Maryland, to Coraopolis, Pennsylvania, in one day on official business. Chalonec left his home at 7:15 a.m. and drove about 62 miles to Baltimore-Washington International Airport, where he parked in a garage. He returned to the parking garage at 6:58 p.m. the same day and drove home, arriving at 8:15 p.m.

Under FTR 301.11-1, a federal employee is eligible for per diem allowance when he/she:

- Performs official travel away from the official station or other areas defined by the agency
- Incurs per diem expenses while performing official travel
- Spends at least 12 hours in travel status.

Chalonec submitted a claim for per diem reimbursement, having spent about 13 hours in travel status. The agency rejected his claim; it had deducted Chalonec's normal commuting time from the time spent in travel status, reducing his time in travel status to 11 hours. Chalonec asked the CBCA to review his agency's decision.

The CBCA found that the agency had acted incorrectly in deducting commuting time from the time spent in travel status. FTR 301-11.9 provides that per diem is calculated from the time an employee departs his or her "home, office, or other authorized point" and ends when the employee returns to his or her home, office, or other authorized point. Under FTR 301-11.10, the employee must record the dates that he or she departs from, and arrives at, the home, office, or authorized point. If the travel occurs within one day, the employee must note that fact on the travel claim.

The CBCA did not find any requirement that an agency deduct commuting time from the calculation of time spent in travel status. Instead, Chalonec had acted in accordance with the FTR by calculating his per diem between the times he left and returned home. The CBCA granted his per diem request.

69 When is travel time considered hours of work?

Compensatory time for travel that includes overtime for hours of work while in a travel status is governed by the rules promulgated by the Office of Personnel Management (OPM) and is a human resources (HR) matter. For example, certain travel time may be creditable as hours of work under the overtime pay provisions in 5 CFR 550.112(g) or 551.422; the rules on travel hours of work depend on whether an employee is covered by or exempt from the Fair Labor Standards Act (FLSA). For FLSA-exempt employees, the crediting of travel time as hours of work is governed under Title 5 rules, in particular, 5 U.S.C. 5542(b)(2) and 5544(a)(3) and 5 CFR 550.112(g) and (j). For FLSA-covered employees, travel time is credited if it is qualifying hours of work under either the Title 5 rules or OPM's FLSA regulations, in particular, 5 CFR 551.401(h) and 551.422. The traveler should contact the agency HR or travel manager to discuss his/her particular situation.

In the case of GSBCA 15326-TRAV, *In the Matter of Edward L. Petersen* (August 8, 2000), a civilian employee of the Department of the Navy in Hansville, Washington, was issued travel orders for temporary duty in Kings Bay, Georgia. Petersen returned from the assignment outside normal work hours. In addition, his flight was delayed.

As a result, the total time Petersen spent returning to his permanent duty station was substantially longer than he had expected.

He submitted a claim for 16 hours of overtime, reflecting the extra time he spent returning from his TDY assignment. The Navy denied the claim. Petersen appealed to the GSBCA.

The board rejected his appeal. It emphasized that any overtime worked by an employee at a TDY assignment cannot qualify as a travel expense. In addition, any dispute regarding the amount of compensation should be submitted to OPM.

70 Is per diem based on a traveler's PDS or official residence?

In some cases a traveler's PDS is not the same as the traveler's actual residence. For example, say a traveler's PDS is Cincinnati, Ohio, but his official residence is Chicago, Illinois, approximately 300 miles away. The traveler commutes daily at his expense from a leased apartment in Cincinnati to his PDS and on weekends to his Chicago residence. If the traveler is sent to Chicago for official business, is his per diem based on departing from Cincinnati or Chicago with a reduced per diem?

FTR section 301-70.200 requires the agency to have established policies and procedures governing when it will pay a reduced per diem. In accordance with FTR section 302-11.100, a traveler's residence is defined as the "one residence from which you regularly commute to and from work on a daily basis." Therefore, the traveler's official travel should be considered from Cincinnati to Chicago in accordance with FTR section 301-11.1 and 300-3.1 unless the agency authorizes a different departure point.

Moreover, administrative mistakes regarding an employee's official duty station cannot serve as the basis for authorizing or calculating per diem. Mistakes do not entitle travelers to reimbursement if the FTR provides otherwise. For example, in GSBCA-15264-TRAV, *In the Matter of Kenneth E. Billings* (May 30, 2000), an employee of the National Credit Union Administration (NCUA) lived and worked in Staunton, Ilinois. His personnel file, however, indicated that his official duty station was Escanaba, Michigan.

NCUA had improperly listed Billings and several other employees as falsely working at various locations to circumvent competitive hiring procedures. A review by OPM discovered the prohibited practices.

NCUA ultimately suspended and demoted several employees involved. Despite knowing of the incorrect designation of his permanent duty station, Billings filed a claim for nearly $20,000 in per diem expenses. He argued that regardless of whether he actually worked or lived in Michigan, that is what was recorded as his official work station on his Standard Form (SF) 50. Therefore, his actual work station in Staunton should be considered a long-term TDY assignment and he should be entitled to two years of per diem for lodging, meals, and mileage expenses. NCUA rejected his argument. Billings appealed to the GSBCA, which was no more understanding.

The board rejected his argument that Escanaba must be considered his permanent work station simply because it was designated on his SF 50. A mistake, due to either administrative error or fraud, cannot serve as the basis for authorizing per diem. The purpose of per diem is to reimburse employees for meals and lodging while away from their homes. Billings had worked and lived in Staunton during the entire time he was employed by NCUA. Except for the improper listing of his official work station, Billings would have no claim to per diem.

The board emphasized that NCUA could not blindly ignore the actual facts of Billings' claim because a government form indicated an opposite conclusion. Permitting reimbursement under such conditions would violate both the letter and spirit of the FTR.

71 Is a traveler required to record departure and arrival dates and times on a travel claim?

A traveler must record the date of departure from, and arrival at, the official station or any other place where travel begins or ends. This same information must be shown for points where the traveler performs TDY or for a stopover or official rest stop location when the arrival or departure affects the per diem allowance or other travel expenses. The traveler should also show the dates for other points visited. Departure and arrival times do not have to be recorded, but the traveler must annotate the travel claim indicating when travel is more than 12 hours but not exceeding 24 hours.

72 If an agency authorizes travelers to depart one day before or after a conference, can it deny reimbursement for expenses incurred for the extra travel day?

FTR section 301.2.2 states in part that an "agency may pay only those expenses essential to the transaction of official business." It is reasonable to assume that the extra day authorized is for the traveler's personal convenience and that the traveler must take appropriate action to ensure that per diem will not be paid prior to finalizing the travel authorization. The agency must deny reimbursement for an extra day of per diem when the extra day is not related to government business.

In GSBCA 14956, *In the Matter of Joseph K. Dunleavy* (June 18, 1999), an employee of the state of New Jersey was authorized to travel to New Mexico to serve as team leader for an environmental compliance assessment survey for the New Mexico National Guard. His agency was responsible for arranging his travel, but his expenses were to be paid by the Department of Defense (DoD).

The survey was scheduled to begin in Santa Fe on July 6 and conclude on July 10. Dunleavy arrived in Albuquerque early, on July 2, and drove to Santa Fe the same day. He returned to New Jersey on July 10. Upon his return, Dunleavy sought per diem reimbursement for July 2 through July 10. DoD refused to reimburse him for July 2 through 5 and instead authorized payment for only July 6 through 10. DoD claimed that it was not necessary for Dunleavy to arrive four days before his assignment started. Dunleavy appealed to the GSBCA.

There was a discrepancy between Dunleavy and his state agency over the events leading to his early departure. According to Dunleavy, he asked his agency to advise him on the costs and availability of flights to Santa Fe arriving on July 5 and departing on July 10. The agency informed him that no flights were available for those days and that he should therefore consider flying to an alternate city.

Dunleavy stated that he called a friend in New Mexico who told him that he should fly into Albuquerque and then drive an hour to Santa Fe. He asked his agency to purchase a ticket to Albuquerque. His agency advised him that no flight was available at government rates for the days in question—the cheapest roundtrip fare was $1,530. The agency informed him that the only possible reservation it could make was for an arrival on July 2. Dunleavy agreed.

In contrast to Dunleavy's account, his agency claimed that he originally requested two round-trip tickets to Santa Fe at government rates with a departure date of July 5 and a return date of July 11, without first requesting advice on costs. DoD's commercial travel office (CTO) informed the state agency that all government rate flights into Santa Fe for the dates requested were booked and that only commercial seats costing over $600 were available.

According to the state travel agent, Dunleavy directed her to purchase the commercial tickets. She explained to him that she could not approve the purchase since there was space available at a government rate of $252 for flights to Albuquerque, which was only 59 miles from Santa Fe. The travel agent said that Dunleavy refused to accept a flight to the alternate city. He instead requested that she check for available flights to Santa Fe at the government rate for earlier arrival dates. After an exhaustive search over several days, the agent found no available flights.

The agent advised Dunleavy that she would not purchase commercial tickets for a flight into Santa Fe on July 5 without confirmation from his program manager. Dunleavy made no attempt to gain approval for an earlier trip from his supervisor; instead, he called the state travel agent after several days and instructed her to book a flight to Albuquerque for July 2. The travel administrator made the arrangements.

GSBCA agreed with DoD's refusal to reimburse Dunleavy per diem for July 2 through July 5. Although the facts surrounding his early departure were disputed, it was Dunleavy's responsibility to provide sufficient evidence that the reason for his early departure was flight availability. Dunleavy, however, failed to provide the board with any documentation that flights to Albuquerque were booked for July 6.

As a result, the board had no choice but to accept the facts presented by his agency. According to those facts, Dunleavy's arrival on July 2 was not "essential for the transaction of official business" and therefore was not compensable since he could have flown to Albuquerque on July 5.

73 What are the per diem entitlements for travel less than 12 hours?

None. Travelers must be in a travel status for more than 12 hours to be paid per diem. Travelers cannot circumvent this requirement by taking a longer route to an assignment, even if done inadvertently.

In GSBCA 15285-TRAV, *In the Matter of Edgardo L. Delgado* (January 9, 2001), an employee of the Farm Service Agency (FSA) in Okmulgee, Oklahoma, was authorized to travel between his permanent duty station and Shawnee, Oklahoma. Delgado departed his home in Tulsa at 5:30 a.m. and drove to Shawnee. Since he was uncertain of the best route to Shawnee from his house, he first drove to his office, without stopping, and then proceeded to Shawnee. He returned home at 5:33 p.m. the same day, slightly more than 12 hours later.

After completing the assignment, Delgado submitted a voucher for mileage reimbursement. He claimed a roundtrip total of 261 miles. In addition, he requested reimbursement for M&IE. FSA refused to reimburse him the total mileage amount or M&IE because he did not take the most direct route. FSA stated that by traveling to his office first, he added unnecessary mileage and time to the trip.

More than 120 miles of his submitted mileage total represented a non-reimbursable commuting distance. In addition, if he had proceeded directly to Shawnee from his home, the total trip time would have been less than 12 hours since he could have departed in the morning at 5:41 a.m. and would have returned at 4:55 p.m. The agency emphasized that employees are eligible for M&IE reimbursement only if they are in travel status for more than 12 hours.

Delgado appealed to the GSBCA, which rejected the appeal. The board noted that the FTR is clear that employees may be reimbursed only when they take the most direct route to an assignment. In this case, Delgado nearly doubled the length of his trip by driving past his office first. Also, the circuitous route added nearly 45 minutes to the trip. An agency should not be obligated to pay for a travel expense that would not have otherwise occurred if an employee had chosen the shortest way to an assignment.

74 What if the travel is more than 12 hours but less than 24 hours?

For travel between 12 and 24 hours, the allowance is 75 percent of the applicable M&IE rate. If overnight lodging is required, reimbursement will cover actual lodging costs not to exceed the maximum lodging rate for the TDY location.

75 What if the travel is 24 hours or more?

For the day of departure, the traveler will receive 75 percent of the applicable M&IE rate; for full days, the traveler will receive 100 percent of the applicable M&IE rate; and on the last day, the traveler will receive 75 percent of the applicable M&IE rate.

76 What are the types of reimbursable per diem expense methods?

The following methods are used to reimburse per diem expenses:

- *Lodging plus* – The per diem allowance for each travel day is established on the basis of the actual amount the traveler pays for lodging, plus an allowance for M&IE, the total of which does not exceed the applicable maximum per diem rate for the location.
- *Actual expense reimbursement* – Payment of authorized actual expenses incurred, up to the limit prescribed by the Administrator of GSA or agency, as appropriate. Entitlement to reimbursement is contingent upon entitlement to per diem and is subject to the same definitions and rules governing per diem.

- *Reduced per diem or flat rate* – A reduced per diem rate authorized by an agency when there are known reductions in lodging and meal costs or when subsistence costs can be determined in advance and are lower than the prescribed per diem rate.
- *Conference allowance* – A predetermined maximum allowance of up to 25 percent greater than the applicable locality lodging portion of the per diem rate. Under this reimbursement method, travelers are reimbursed the actual amount incurred for lodging up to the conference lodging allowance.

77 When can a traveler claim actual expense reimbursement instead of the standard per diem rate?

If a traveler's approved per diem is insufficient, the traveler may request reimbursement for actual expenses for either lodging or meals or both. Specific authorization or prior approval is required for payment of actual expenses in accordance with FTR section 301-2.5(j). However, agency policy may allow an "after-the-fact" approval in accordance with FTR section 301-11.302.

A traveler may request actual expense reimbursement in advance when:

- Lodging or meals are procured at a prearranged place such as a hotel where a meeting, conference, or training session is held
- Costs have escalated because of special events (e.g., missile launching periods, sporting events, World's Fair, conventions, natural or manmade disasters); lodging and meal expenses within prescribed allowances cannot be obtained nearby; and costs to commute to and from the nearby location consume most or all of the savings achieved from occupying less expensive lodging
- The TDY location is subject to a presidentially declared disaster and the agency has issued a blanket actual expense authorization for the affected location
- The agency deems it appropriate based on mission requirements or for any other reason, including post-travel approval when necessary and authorized.

78 Is per diem based on the TDY or lodging location?

Per diem is determined based on the traveler's TDY location and not the traveler's lodging location. Per diem rates are established for the TDY location. The traveler may sleep anywhere but must perform TDY at a specific location.

In GSBCA 13684-TRAV, *In the Matter of Mark Chapman* (April 9, 1997), a civilian employee of DoD in California was authorized for a TDY assignment in Patuxent River, Maryland. His travel orders provided that he would fly from San Diego to Washington, D.C., and then drive to Patuxent River.

Chapman's travel office informed him that he could stay in Washington on arriving and proceed to Patuxent River the next morning. Since his TDY was scheduled to conclude on a Friday, the office also advised him that he could stay in Washington on Saturday and Sunday nights before returning to San Diego on Monday morning.

Chapman followed that advice. Upon his return, he submitted a voucher for his expenses. DoD refused to reimburse him for the full costs of the three hotel nights in Washington, limiting reimbursement for those nights to the cost of a hotel in Patuxent River. Chapman appealed to the GSBCA.

The board rejected his appeal, noting that the JTR provides that employees must obtain lodging at the TDY location. If the employee chooses to stay at a hotel away from that location because of a personal preference or convenience, the allowable per diem is limited to the maximum per diem rate for the TDY location.

Chapman explained his stay in Washington as a way to avoid traffic and driving after a long flight. Because these reasons benefited Chapman rather than DoD, his stay must be considered for his personal convenience. Although his travel office advised him that he could stay over in Washington, that advice was contrary to the JTR and therefore could not be the basis for reimbursement.

79 How is per diem calculated if travel is interrupted because of illness, incapacitation, or hospitalization?

FTR section 301-70.501 allows the continuance of per diem "when an employee interrupts a travel assignment because of an incapacitating illness or injury." FTR section 301-70.502 prohibits reimbursement if "confinement in a hospital or medical facility that is within the proximity of the official station or that is the same one the employee would have been admitted to if the illness or injury had occurred while at the official station and/or the government provides or reimburses the employee for hospitalization under any federal statute (including hospitalization in a Department of Veterans Affairs (VA) medical center or military hospital) other than 5 U.S.C. 8901-8913 (Federal Employees Health Benefits Program)."

In GSBCA 14523-TRAV, *In the Matter of Harold Lee* (June 16, 1998), an employee of the Department of Transportation (DOT) suffered an incapacitating illness that required hospitalization while he was on TDY. Lee's health insurance under the Civilian Health and Medical Program of the Uniformed Services (CHAMPUS) covered his hospitalization. DOT subsequently asked the GSBCA to rule on whether Lee was entitled to per diem reimbursement for the hospitalization period. The board determined that the FTR and the JTR specifically prohibit reimbursement for per diem expenses when the employee "receives hospitalization (or is reimbursed for hospital expenses) under any federal statute . . . other than 5 U.S.C. 8901-8913." Since Lee received his hospitalization under health insurance obtained under CHAMPUS, not the Federal Employees Health Benefits Progam, he was not entitled to per diem reimbursement.

Special Needs

Special needs are physical characteristics of a traveler that are not necessarily defined as a disability. Such physical characteristics could include, for example, the weight or height of the traveler. The government's general policy is to provide reasonable accommodations to an employee with a special need by paying for additional travel expenses incurred.

80 Under what conditions will an agency pay additional travel expenses to accommodate a special need?

An agency will pay additional travel expenses that are incurred to accommodate a special physical need that is either clearly visible and discernible or is substantiated in writing by a competent medical authority.

81 What additional travel expenses may an agency pay to accommodate a special need?

An agency's approving official may pay any expenses deemed necessary to accommodate an employee with a special need, including (but not limited to):

- Transportation and per diem expenses incurred by a family member or other attendant who must travel with the federal employee to make the trip possible
- Specialized transportation to, from, or at the TDY duty location
- Specialized services provided by a common carrier to accommodate the special need
- Costs for handling baggage that are a direct result of the special need
- Renting or transporting a wheelchair
- Other than coach-class accommodations to accommodate the special need, under FTR Subpart B of Part 301-10 (Common Carrier Transportation)
- Services of an attendant, when necessary, to accommodate the special need. (For limits on the amount that may be paid to an attendant, other than travel expenses, see 5 U.S.C. 3102 and guidance at http://www.opm.gov/disability/mngr_6-01-B.asp.)

Interviewee Travel

To recruit highly qualified individuals, agencies may pay pre-employment interview travel expenses. The interviewee will be entitled to expenses as if he/she were a government employee traveling on official business. Pre-employment interview expenses include travel to attend confirmation hearings. Pre-employment travel expenses may not be authorized to offset or defray other expenses that are not allowable for an interviewee.

Prior to paying pre-employment travel expenses, agencies it must establish policies and procedures governing:

- When pre-employment interview travel expenses will be paid, including the criteria for determining which individuals or positions qualify for payment
- Who will determine, in each individual case, that a person qualifies for pre-employment interview travel expenses
- Who will determine what expenses will be paid for each individual interviewee.

Agencies must also:

- Provide interviewees with a list of FEMA-approved accommodations in the vicinity of the interview and encourage them to stay in an approved accommodation
- Inform the interviewee that he/she is responsible for excess costs and any additional expenses that he/she incurs for personal preference or convenience
- Inform the interviewee that the government will not pay for excess costs resulting from circuitous routes, delays, or luxury accommodations or services unnecessary or unjustified in the performance of official business
- Assist the interviewee in preparing the travel claim
- Provide the interviewee with instructions on how to submit the claim
- Inform the interviewee that he/she may be subject to criminal penalties if he/she knowingly presents a false, fictitious, or fraudulent travel claim (see 18 U.S.C. 287 and 1001).

Not having or following established policies and procedures could lead to misunderstandings between the agency and interviewee, and possibly denial of travel expenses for the interviewee. For example, in CBCA 1620-TRAV, *In the Matter of Westley K. Collins* (February 24, 2010), a federal employee of the Department of Energy in Oregon applied for a position with the Federal Aviation Administration (FAA) in Renton,

Washington. The FAA called Collins to set up an interview. What happened next was the subject of a dispute between the two parties.

The FAA contended that it initially proposed to interview Collins by phone, but Collins responded that he would be in the area visiting a friend and would prefer a face-to-face interview. The FAA then set up an in-person interview. Collins maintained that the option of a telephone interview never came up, and he was instead scheduled for an in-person interview. He said that he was willing to travel to Renton and arranged to stay with a friend to minimize the expense to the agency. Both parties agreed that they did not discuss the reimbursement of Collins' travel expenses.

Collins was interviewed for the position on November 4, 2008. He was informed by letter dated November 15, 2008, that he had not been selected for the position. Collins responded by letter, asking, among other things, about paperwork to submit a travel claim. He never received a response.

On April 15, 2009, Collins wrote another letter to the interviewer asking how to file his travel expense claim. The FAA responded in an April 23, 2009, letter, stating that travel expenses would not be paid. The FAA noted that it had not been aware that Collins had expected to be reimbursed for the in-person interview, and it had never agreed to pay his travel costs. Additionally, the FAA noted that it believed that it was simply accommodating Collins' preference in holding the interview in person. The agency said that if Collins had broached the subject of repayment when they were setting up the interview, a telephone interview would have arranged instead.

Collins appealed to the CBCA.

The FAA Travel Policy, the agency's governing travel regulation, provides that the FAA may, but is not required to, authorize an allowance for pre-employment interview expenses when it has determined that reimbursement will facilitate the recruitment of highly qualified individuals (FAATP sections 301-32.1 to 301-21.3). The guidance provides that when travel expenses are authorized, the interviewee should not purchase his/her own ticket; instead, the interviewing office will either provide a ticket or permit the interviewee to arrange travel through the FAA's travel management system (FAATP 302-32.203).

In this case, Collins purchased his own ticket, an indication that reimbursement was not authorized.

The FAA Travel Policy is consistent with the FTR, which provides guidance on the payment of pre-employment interview travel expenses at section 301-75. The FTR provides that a federal agency may pay pre-employment interview travel expenses if it determines that it is in the best interest of the government to do so (FTR section 301-75.2). FTR section 301-75.3 specifies that federal agencies must establish policies and procedures governing:

- When to pay pre-employment interview travel expenses, including the criteria for determining which individuals or positions qualify for payment of such expenses
- Who will determine, in each individual case, that a person qualifies for pre-employment interview travel expenses
- Who will determine what expenses will be paid for each individual interviewee.

Collins argued that because he is already a federal employee, albeit with another agency, his interview should not have been treated as a "pre-employment" interview. The CBCA disagreed, stating that "since Mr. Collins was not already employed by the FAA, his interview was properly categorized as a pre-employment interview."

Ultimately, the CBCA supported the FAA's decision not to reimburse Collins' travel expenses, noting that "the FAA simply did not authorize reimbursement of Mr. Collins' travel expenses. There is no statute or regulation that required that it do so. Thus the claim was properly denied."

82 May employees be reimbursed for traveling to interview with another agency if they are seeking a new position as a result of a reduction in force?

Reimbursement is at the discretion of the employee's current agency. Over the past several years, downsizing has become a way of life for federal employees. Some casualties of reduction in force (RIF) actions have been absorbed into new positions with new agencies.

Individuals who have found different positions within the government, however, have often done so at significant personal costs, specifically time and travel for interviews. In a GSBCA decision, one employee learned when reimbursement is permissible.

In GSBCA 14312-TRAV, *In the Matter of Sandra L. Roberts* (November 10, 1998), after receiving a RIF notice, Roberts, a civilian employee of the Defense Finance Accounting Service (DFAS) in Detroit, Michigan, applied for a position with the Department of Justice (DOJ) in Washington, D.C. As part of the application process, Roberts traveled to Washington, at the request of DOJ, for an interview. DOJ informed Roberts that it would not pay for her travel expenses, so Roberts requested that DFAS reimburse the costs. She argued that the expenses were similar to the relocation costs that were normally paid by DFAS.

DFAS refused to reimburse her. It noted that she had not been issued travel orders for her interview. Moreover, she should seek reimbursement from DOJ since pre-employment interview travel is a "discretionary entitlement granted by the interviewing agency." Roberts appealed to the GSBCA.

The board agreed with DFAS's decision. It noted that section 5706(b) of Title 5 of the U.S. Code permits, but does not require, agencies to reimburse interviewees for pre-employment travel expenses. According to the board, "it was within the complete discretion of DFAS to deny those expenses."

The board was not persuaded by Roberts' comparison of the travel costs to relocation expenses. In addition, it found no statutory authority to support Roberts' argument that her employing agency (DFAS) rather than the interviewing agency (DOJ) should be responsible for interview travel costs.

Invitational Travel

Invitational travel is authorized travel by non-federal government employees who are acting in a capacity directly related to or in connection with official government activities.

83 What are the rules for invitational travel reimbursement?

Reimbursement for travel by non-federal government employees is subject to the same regulations as travel by federal employees. Invitational travelers should use the centrally billed account for the purchase of common carrier tickets and should not be provided an advance of funds.

84 Can an employee accept monies from a non-federal source for invitational travel?

No. Under 31 U.S.C. 1353, employees and their spouses are prohibited from accepting cash or checks made payable to the employee or spouse from a non-federal source for travel or attendance at meetings or similar functions.

PART V

While on Travel

The government may pay only those expenses essential to the transaction of official business. Individuals must be in a travel status as defined in the Per Diem section of *Part IV, Before You Travel,* to be entitled to allowances and expenses. While performing official travel, a federal employee is allowed to incur certain travel and travel-related expenses.

A contractor-issued government travel charge card is the government's preferred method of paying travel expenses. To assist cardholders on how to use the travel charge card responsibly, this part provides information on cardholder responsibilities, the do's and don'ts of using the travel charge card, and actions the agency may take against the cardholder for misuse or abuse of the travel charge card.

The role of an agency/organization program coordinator (A/OPC) is important. The A/OPC manages the agency's travel charge card program and authorized cardholders. A/OPC responsibilities, helpful hints for reducing delinquency, and best practices for managing both the agency's travel charge card program and cardholders are also provided in this part.

Once the traveler has been directed to travel, has obtained authorization to travel, and is on official travel, the traveler may then incur travel and travel-related expenses. The government may pay only those expenses that are essential to the transaction of official business. This part also provides information on allowable expenses for transportation, lodging, meals, and incidentals.

For expenses that are not mentioned, consult the FTR and your agency travel manager for guidance.

PAYING FOR TRAVEL EXPENSES WITH A CONTRACTOR-ISSUED GOVERNMENT TRAVEL CHARGE CARD

The Travel and Transportation Reform Act (TTRA) of 1998 mandates that federal employees use the government contractor-issued travel charge card for all payments of expenses related to official government travel unless an exemption has been granted in accordance with the FTR. The purposes of the government-wide travel charge card program are to: (1) provide commercial charge cards and associated services in support of official domestic and international federal government travel and travel-related expenses; (2) streamline the travel process by allowing employees to purchase negotiated tickets and book hotels and rental cars through their travel management center and commercial travel office; (3) improve government operations by simplifying the financial process; and (4) provide a platform for improving government operations and accountability.

The A/OPC is the individual responsible for managing and overseeing the travel charge card program within each agency. That individual serves as the liaison with the travel charge card contractor or issuing bank, management, and agency contacts such as the finance office and transaction dispute office.

A/OPC Responsibilities

The GSA SmartPay2 Master Contract lists the A/OPC's responsibilities, which include:

- Maintain an up-to-date list of account names, account numbers, addresses, emails, and phone numbers of all current cardholders and accounts
- Provide to the issuing bank any changes in the agency's organizational structure that may affect invoice/report distribution
- Review and evaluate the bank's technical and administrative task order performance and compliance
- Resolve technical and operational problems between the bank and cardholders as required

- Take appropriate action regarding delinquent accounts and report to internal investigative units and the GSA contracting officer any observed violations of applicable executive orders, laws, or regulations
- Participate in training conferences and train cardholders
- Ensure that cardholders use the charge card correctly
- Monitor account activity and manage delinquencies
- Ensure that appropriate steps are taken to mitigate suspension or cancellation actions
- Develop agency program procedures and policies as necessary.

85 What are some best practices for managing cardholders?

With the support of the agency head, the A/OPC should:

- Train cardholders in accordance with Appendix B on the proper use of the travel charge card, including ethics training. Develop a traveler hotline to respond to cardholder questions.
- Develop and maintain a travel-specific website for the agency.
- Publish answers to frequently asked questions related to travel on the agency website.
- Create an informational newsletter.
- Send periodic reminders to cardholders on agency travel policies and procedures.
- Hold orientation sessions with new cardholders.
- Provide cardholder training on how to fill out a proper travel claim/voucher.
- Remind cardholders who are on extended travel to submit interim travel claims/vouchers to ensure timely receipt of reimbursement.
- Notify cardholders that their obligation to pay their respective bank by the billing due date is not contingent upon receipt of a travel reimbursement from the agency/organization.

- Contact cardholders who appear on the pre-suspension/pre-cancellation report by phone, email, or correspondence. Advise cardholders that immediate action must be taken.
- Use a statement insert/statement message provided by the bank to convey information to cardholders.
- Provide the GSA SmartPay2 card-sized brochure, *Helpful Hints for Travel Card Use*.
- Send an annual letter from your agency director reminding cardholders of their responsibilities.
- Provide a travel charge card training video for cardholders.

86 What are some best practices for A/OPC program management?

A/OPCs should follow these best practices:

- Use online tools provided by the banks, GSA, and your agency.
- Email updates to A/OPCs at all levels regarding program changes.
- Review reports regularly and track trends in delinquency rates and charge-offs/write-offs.
- Use exception reports to detect misuse of the travel charge card or unusual spending patterns.
- Use ad hoc reporting tools provided by your bank to customize or develop your own agency reports.
- Eliminate manual calculations by developing ad hoc reports that can be generated as needed.
- Ensure that cardholder information is properly secured and confidentially maintained in accordance with your agency's security and privacy regulations as well as with the Privacy Act. Create a monthly newsletter/memorandum to reinforce agency travel charge cardholder policies for misuse or account delinquency.
- Develop and implement an agency-established penalty guide with your agency's human resources office outlining appropriate disciplinary action for undisputed delinquencies and non-official use of the travel charge card by employees.

- Perform an annual review of all issued cards to determine whether each card meets the criteria for continued participation in the federal government travel charge card program.

87 What actions can an A/OPC take to help manage the agency's travel card program in a way that prevents abuse, minimizes risk, and eliminates or reduces delinquencies?

An A/OPC can take several preventive actions to help manage and minimize risk in the agency's charge card program. These include:

- Reviewing the credit limits of cardholders to determine what is appropriate based on the frequency of travel
- Deactivating cards when not in use
- Establishing ATM withdrawal limits
- Monitoring delinquency and unauthorized charges more effectively by decreasing the number of days for suspension, cancellation, or late fees
- Blocking certain merchant category codes to prevent unauthorized use.
- Suspending or canceling a card for inappropriate use or failing to pay the bank on time
- Implementing salary offset
- Ensuring the use of split disbursement
- Reviewing accounts periodically to ensure that all unused travel charge cards are closed (including accounts for employees who have left the agency)
- Reporting delinquency and misuse/abuse to the appropriate officials.

Cardholder Responsibilities

Cardholders should be aware that there is a difference between what we generally know as a credit card, which is most likely what you use personally, and a charge card. Unlike a credit card, the government charge card does not extend credit. A charge card requires payment in full upon receipt of the bill.

The cardholder's responsibilities include, but are not limited to:

- Understanding individual agency/organization policies and procedures as they relate to official federal government travel
- Paying all charges and fees associated with the individually billed account (IBA) travel charge card in full by the billing due date (whether or not the cardholder has been reimbursed by the agency)
- Complying with the terms and conditions of the cardholder account agreement that is issued with the travel charge card by the bank.

Public Law 109-115 requires agencies to perform a creditworthiness evaluation prior to issuing a travel charge card to first-time applicants. OMB Circular A-123, Appendix B, requires training and refresher training on travel card management for all participants in the government charge card program. This includes cardholders, A/OPCs, approving officials, and other accountable/billing officials.

88 Can a contract fare be used for personal travel and the ticket paid using a personal credit card, or can a government travel charge card be used to pay for the entire trip and the personal portion not be vouchered?

No. The government travel charge card may not be used for personal travel. Government contract fares may not be used for any personal leg of the trip or to calculate a difference in fares for the personal travel.

89 Who and what expenses may be exempted from mandatory use of the government travel charge card and who is authorized to provide the exemption?

The Administrator of General Services will exempt any payment, person, type, or class of payments, or type or class of personnel in any case in which—

- It is in the best interest of the United States to do so
- Payment through a travel charge card is impractical or imposes unreasonable burdens or costs on federal employees or federal agencies
- The Secretary of Defense or the Secretary of Homeland Security requests an exemption for the members of the uniformed services.

The head of a federal agency or his/her designee may exempt any payment, person, type, or class of payments, or type or class of agency personnel if the exemption is determined to be necessary in the interest of the agency. The Administrator of General Services must be notified in writing within 30 days after granting the exemption, stating the reasons for the exemption.

90 What expenses are exempt from mandatory use of the government travel charge card?

The Administrator of General Services exempts the following from mandatory use of the government contractor-issued travel charge card:

- Expenses incurred at a vendor that does not accept the government contractor–issued travel charge card
- Laundry/dry cleaning
- Parking
- Local transportation
- Taxi

- Tips
- Meals (when use of the card is impractical, e.g., group meals, where the government contractor-issued travel charge card is not accepted)
- Phone calls (when a government calling card is available for use in accordance with agency policy)
- Employee who has an application pending for the travel charge card
- Individuals traveling on invitational travel
- New appointees
- Relocation allowances prescribed in 41 CFR Chapter 302, except en-route travel and househunting trip expenses
- Employees who travel five times or fewer a year (although agencies have the discretion to issue a travel charge card to such employees).

91 Can a traveler be reimbursed for fees while authorized to use the travel charge card for an advance?

Yes. A traveler may be reimbursed for fees for using an ATM and to obtain traveler's checks, money orders, or certified checks. However, the reimbursement for transaction fees is applicable only to the government travel charge card and not to a traveler's personal credit or charge card.

In CBCA 972-TRAV, *In the Matter of Deborah E. Kenney* (March 10, 2008), a civilian DoD employee traveled to Cotonou, Benin, for an initial conference planning meeting. Kenney's travel orders specified that she was to obtain cash from an ATM using her government travel card. The conference coordinator further advised her that she would need to carry cash in new colored bills and that she should not use credit cards because credit card numbers are regularly stolen in Benin.

Kenney had a credit limit of $5,000 on her government charge card—and an unpaid balance of $4,448.93. She was unable to raise her credit limit before her trip, and she did not make a payment on her government card. Instead, Kenney took a $3,000 cash advance from her personal credit card.

The agency reimbursed Kenney for the $3,000 in cash, but not for a $90 transaction fee charged by her bank for the extension of credit. Upon review of the situation, the CBCA determined that the agency was correct in not reimbursing the $90 transaction fee.

Use of the government travel card is mandatory for all DoD personnel for expenses arising from official government travel, unless otherwise exempted, under DoD Financial Management Regulation section 0301 (Sept. 2000). The CBCA noted that DoD benefits from this policy through improved cash management practices and reduced administrative workloads. In addition, it receives rebates based upon usage from the company that issues the travel cards. To encourage government travelers to use the government-issued charge cards, the federal government reimburses administrative fees when government-sponsored cards are used.

The CBCA pointed out that Kenney could have asked for her travel authorization to be amended to exempt her from having to use the government travel card and authorize her to secure cash from her personal credit card. Had she done so, the transaction fee might have been a reimbursable transaction fee. Lacking the proper authorization, her claim could not be reimbursed.

92 Can a traveler submit a voucher in advance of travel to pay a credit card charge for a room deposit?

Yes. FTR section 301-11.32 states that "your agency may reimburse you for an advance room deposit, when such a deposit is required by the lodging facility to secure a room reservation, prior to the beginning of your scheduled official travel. However, if you are reimbursed the advance room deposit, but fail to perform the scheduled official travel for reasons not acceptable to your agency, resulting in forfeit of the deposit, you are indebted to the government for that amount and must repay it in a manner prescribed by your agency."

93 Can the government travel charge card be used in the vicinity of a traveler's permanent duty station?

The GSA SmartPay2 master contract allows an option for non-DoD customer organizations to permit use of the travel charge card for local travel in accordance with agency policies and procedures. To assist agencies that intend to use the travel charge card for local travel, the Office of Charge Card Management (OCCM) has developed a local travel management plan template that includes items to consider when developing policies and procedures. The template will assist agencies in outlining implementation details and proper controls and oversight for use of the travel charge card for local travel. For more information, see GSA SmartPay Bulletin No. 14, (November 2, 2010), https://smartpay.gsa.gov/news/smart-bulletins.

94 If a traveler is not authorized to receive a government travel charge card but is required to travel, how can the traveler pay for travel expenses?

An agency may authorize one or a combination of the following methods of payment:

- Personal funds, including cash or personal charge card
- Travel advances
- Government transportation request (GTR), which is another method of procuring passenger transportation services in certain travel situations (managed by the agency travel manager).

95 Can a traveler use his/her government travel charge card to pay for a co-worker's lodging and dining expenses?

No. A cardholder who uses his/her government travel charge card to pay for a co-worker's lodging or dining expense cannot submit a voucher for that traveler's expense. Such a transaction is viewed as a personal transaction between the cardholder and the co-worker; the cardholder would need to seek repayment from the co-worker. The cardholder is solely responsible for payment of expenses as reflected on his/her charge card statement and any liability that may occur if the co-worker does not reimburse the cardholder for the expenses since the cardholder will not be allowed to claim those expenses on his/her voucher. The cardholder may also be subject to disciplinary action if the agency determines such use to be "misuse."

96 What is considered misuse/abuse and fraudulent use of a government travel charge card?

Intentional use of a government charge card for other than official government business constitutes misuse and, depending on the situation, may constitute fraud.

97 What actions by the cardholder could be considered misuse or abuse?

Examples of misuse/abuse include:

- Personal use
- Use of the travel charge card for someone other than the specific cardholder
- Use while not on official government travel
- Use locally, if not on official government travel status under a travel order/authorization
- Purchases from an unauthorized merchant
- Excessive ATM withdrawals
- Failure to pay undisputed amounts on time.

98 What are the consequences for misuse of a government travel charge card?

The consequences may include:

- Reprimand
- Travel charge card cancellation
- Counseling

- Suspension of employment
- Termination of employment
- Criminal prosecution.

99 What are some helpful hints for cardholders regarding travel card use?

Tips for cardholders include:

- **Do** use your government travel charge card to pay for official travel expenses.
- **Do** obtain travel advances for official travel through an ATM if authorized by your agency.
- **Do** track your expenses and keep receipts while on travel so you have accurate information for filing your travel claim.
- **Do** file your travel claim within five days after you complete your trip or every 30 days if you are on continuous travel.
- **Do** submit payment in full for each monthly bill.
- **Do** follow your bank's dispute process for incorrect charges.
- **Do** call your bank's customer service number if you have questions about your monthly bill.
- **Do** be aware that misuse of the travel charge card can result in disciplinary actions by your agency.
- **Do** be aware that failure to pay your bill in a timely manner can result in suspension or cancellation of your card.
- **Do** return your travel charge card to your A/OPC to be destroyed if you leave your agency or retire.
- **Do** immediately report your lost or stolen card to your A/OPC and the card-issuing bank.
- **Do** destroy any lost or stolen cards that are recovered.
- **Do** be aware of identity theft schemes attempting to gain access to financial information.
- **Don't** use your travel charge card for personal use.
- **Don't** obtain travel advances through the ATM that exceed your expected out-of-pocket expenditures for a trip.

- **Don't** obtain travel advances through the ATM unless you are on travel or will be on travel shortly.
- **Don't** allow your monthly bill to become overdue because this could result in suspension or cancellation of your card.
- **Don't** wait for receipt of your monthly billing statement to file your travel claim.
- **Don't** forget that the card is issued in your name and liability for payment is your responsibility.
- **Don't** write your personal identification number (PIN) on your card or carry your PIN in your wallet.

100 If a supervisor directs a traveler to purchase an item unrelated to the traveler's purpose of travel on the traveler's government travel charge card, what action can the traveler take without fear of being insubordinate?

On January 15, 2009, OMB issued a revision to Appendix B of OMB Circular A-123. The revision added a requirement to Section 4.8 that states in part that "where an official directs an erroneous purchase to be made by a cardholder or directs a cardholder to purchase items or services that are subsequently determined to be improper, the official who directed the purchase shall, in accordance with agency policy: (a) reimburse the government and (b) be subject to disciplinary action."

The traveler should contact his/her A/OPC or agency official for further guidance. Otherwise, the traveler could be subject to the agency's disciplinary action under FTR sections 301-51.6 and 301-51.7.

101 If on official travel and there is a government-wide shutdown, can a traveler continue to use the government travel charge card?

Under most circumstances, in the absence of appropriations and if the traveler is not an "excepted" employee, the traveler is no longer traveling on official business. Therefore, the traveler is prohibited from incurring any obligations and must return either before a lapse in appropriations or as soon as possible. However, if the agency has identified the traveler as an "excepted" employee and the traveler meets one of the stringent exceptions for incurring an obligation in the absence of agency appropriations (such as emergency travel for the protection of life and property), the traveler may continue to use the travel charge card.

Travelers should review their agency's policy and procedures for a government-wide shutdown to determine whether or not they are an excepted employee and then follow agency procedures. Travelers should also contact their agency's travel manager for further guidance.

INCURRING TRAVEL EXPENSES

The government may pay only those expenses that are essential to the transaction of official business to accomplish the travel mission. Administering the authorization and payment of travel expenses in accordance with the FTR and agency travel policy generally involves:

- Limiting the authorization and payment of travel expenses to travel that is necessary to accomplish the traveler's mission in the most economical and effective manner
- Considering budget constraints, adherence to travel policies, and reasonableness of expenses
- Considering alternatives, including teleconferencing, prior to authorizing travel.

102 If a supervisor authorizes the employee to make a purchase verbally, can the agency later deny the claim?

The travel authorization is a record of vested travel entitlements. It provides a notice and record of the employee's instructions and entitlements and may not be administratively altered after the fact to increase or decrease benefits in the absence of clear error. Therefore, travel orders, either written or verbal (since post-authorization may be approved after-the-fact travel), that are contrary to law or regulation cannot create a right to reimbursement where none exists.

For example, an employee was required to travel from Alabama to California on official travel to represent the agency on a technical panel and attend two scheduled meetings. The employee's luggage did not arrive at the TDY destination. The employee contacted her supervisor and was provided verbal authorization to purchase toiletries and two dresses. However, when the employee submitted her voucher for the expenses as a miscellaneous expense, the claim was denied by Finance.

Unless the agency has specific provisions under its appropriations act or other legislation, it may not use appropriated funds to purchase toiletries and articles of personal clothing that may be retained for personal use. Such items are not considered essential for accomplishing official travel and are therefore considered an unauthorized expense.

FTR section 301-52.8 provides the authority for an approving official to disallow an expense. Also, disbursing and certifying officials assume the ultimate responsibility under 31 U.S.C. 3528 for the validity of the claim as stated in FTR section 301-71.203.

In CBCA 2120-TRAV, *In the Matter of Brian T. Harris* (Jan. 7, 2011), a civilian employee of the Department of the Navy was issued travel orders to attend a conference in Manchester, England. According to the employee, his baggage was lost for 48 hours. To ensure he was dressed in proper business attire for the conference, he purchased shoes, socks, pants, a shirt, and a tie, at a total cost of $248.21.

After receiving no reimbursement from the airline that lost his baggage, Harris filed a claim with the Navy for reimbursement under the Military Personnel and Civilian Employee Claims Act (31 U.S.C. 3721 (2006)). The Navy denied his claim. Harris appealed to the CBCA, asking the board to consider his claim for reimbursement.

Although the CBCA does not have jurisdiction to review claims under the Employee Claims Act, it considered whether Harris could be reimbursed under federal travel policy. Unfortunately for Harris, no provision in the FTR or JTR provides for reimbursement of costs to replace items lost during the course of travel.

103 Is an employee allowed to have family or other dependents travel with him/her on official TDY travel?

The employee always has the option of bringing family members or other dependents on travel, but the government does not assume liability for the employee's family or dependents. If the employee chooses to travel with family or dependents, the employee will be reimbursed as if the employee traveled alone.

However, if the employee travels with another employee who is a member of the employee's immediate family and also is traveling on official business, the two employees will be treated as unrelated employees and each will receive reimbursement for transportation and subsistence.

104 Since government travelers are allowed to mix personal and official travel, can a traveler schedule return travel on the next business day if the official travel ends on a weekend?

Federal employees are normally expected to schedule official travel on business days, but exceptions may be made. For example, if an employee completes his/her TDY assignment late on a Friday afternoon, the travel regulations permit the employee to wait until Saturday to return rather than leave late on Friday evening. The employee, however, may not wait until the next official business day, for example, Monday, to travel.

In GSBCA 14920-TRAV, *In the Matter of David L. Butcher* (August 31, 1999), a civilian employee of the Department of the Navy in Washington, D.C., was issued travel orders for TDY in California. His TDY ended on Friday afternoon but his orders permitted him to remain in California through the weekend and return on Monday.

Upon his return, Butcher submitted a travel voucher for his hotel, meals, and rental car costs, including those for the weekend following completion of his TDY. Butcher was reimbursed for all of his expenses during his TDY, including the costs of a hotel for

Friday evening. In addition, he was reimbursed for the majority of his meal and incidental costs for Saturday. He was not reimbursed for his Saturday and Sunday evening lodging expenses nor his meal and incidental expenses for Sunday and Monday morning.

The Defense Finance Accounting Service (DFAS) informed Butcher that his orders should not have authorized him to stay until Monday. It noted that the JTR requires employees to return no later than the day after completing a TDY, even if that day is a Saturday or Sunday. The agency explained that it normally catches these mistakes, but in this instance it failed to do so. While it believed he was entitled to reimbursement since his extended stay was the result of incorrect travel orders, the JTR precluded it from honoring that portion of his voucher.

Butcher appealed to the GSBCA. The board rejected his claim, noting that paragraph C1058-B.3 of the JTR prohibits employees from delaying their return from a TDY through a weekend. At best, if an employee completes the TDY late Friday afternoon, as in this case, the employee may return the following day. An agency is authorized to reimburse the employee for Friday evening lodging and meal expenses.

In addition, an agency may pay up to 75 percent of the employee's meal and incidental expenses for Saturday. All other expenses are the responsibility of the employee. The board sympathized with Butcher's circumstances. Although it recognized that his travel orders erroneously permitted him to stay through the weekend, his good-faith reliance on those orders did not provide him a basis for recovery.

105 What is the maximum amount a traveler can be reimbursed for parking a car at the airport?

Parking fees at an airport may not exceed the cost of a roundtrip taxi fare, even in the case of an emergency.

The traveler must exercise the same care in incurring expenses that a prudent person would exercise if traveling on personal business (FTR section 301-2.3). Otherwise, the traveler will be responsible for expenses over the reimbursement limits established by the agency. The agency has discretion to determine whether or not the expense is excessive (FTR section 301-2.4) and may reimburse the traveler in accordance with FTR section 301-10.308, which states "Your agency may reimburse your parking fee as an allowable transportation expense not to exceed the cost of taxi fare to/from the terminal."

In GSBCA 13965-TRAV, *In the Matter of Arthur A. Johnson* (February 26, 1997), a civilian employee of the Coast Guard in Alexandria, Virginia, was authorized to attend a conference in Hawaii. He was scheduled to depart from Ronald Reagan Airport.

Due to a major blizzard, Johnson was unable to take a taxi to the airport. Instead, he drove his own car and parked it at the airport. The total parking cost was $114.60. He submitted a voucher for the expense.

The Coast Guard limited reimbursement to $41.40, the cost of a round-trip taxi fare. Johnson appealed to the GSBCA, arguing that an exception to the FTR limits should be made in an emergency. The board disagreed, concluding that no exceptions exist under the FTR.

106 Can a traveler be reimbursed for unconverted foreign currency that could not be converted back to U.S. dollars?

Yes. Under certain circumstances, the inability to convert foreign currency back to U.S. dollars qualifies as a reimbursable expense.

In GSBCA-15242-TRAV, *In the Matter of Lemuel E. Mauldin, III* (March 27, 2000), an employee of the National Aeronautics and Space Administration (NASA) was on official travel to the Ukraine and Russia. NASA gave Mauldin a travel advance of $3,140, which he deposited into his checking account. He withdrew approximately $2,000 of the advance in U.S. currency to take with him. He converted $440 into Ukrainian currency since he anticipated using approximately $90 worth of Ukrainian currency to pay a charge for excess baggage.

Mauldin knew from prior experience that he would be required to pay for excess baggage with local currency since credit cards would not be accepted. Upon his departure, Mauldin was not charged for excess baggage. As a result, he did not spend the Ukrainian currency. He attempted to convert it back to U.S. dollars at the airport; however, no banks were available.

Mauldin carried the currency to his next destination, Russia, where he made several unsuccessful attempts to convert the currency. Upon arrival back in the United States, he made three more attempts to convert the currency, but no banks would accept it. Mauldin submitted a travel voucher shortly after his return. He included the currency with his voucher, noting that the currency was attached. He requested reimbursement of $5,992.46, including $90 for the Ukrainian currency.

NASA reimbursed Mauldin all his expenses except the $90 foreign currency. The agency determined it was an "exchange loss" and claimed it returned the Ukrainian currency. Mauldin denied that the foreign currency was returned and requested an adjudication.

NASA denied Mauldin's appeal on two grounds: (1) reimbursement was properly disallowed as an exchange loss and (2) the employee failed to safeguard his travel advance, i.e., he had lost the money after it was returned. Mauldin appealed to the GSBCA.

The board disagreed with NASA's decision. It noted that the $90 should not be considered an exchange loss. An exchange loss has traditionally been defined as the "loss an employee sustains in converting foreign currency into U.S. dollars by reason of variation in the basic value of the dollar during the time the employee held the currency." In this situation, Mauldin was not trying to recover the variation in value due to fluctuation in currency but instead was seeking reimbursement for holding unconverted foreign currency.

The board also determined that Mauldin had not lost the Ukrainian currency. In its opinion, NASA had never returned the money to him. Because the money was lost while in the custody and control of the government, its loss should be borne by the government.

The board cited a 1981 Comptroller General decision (B-200404, February 12, 1981) that held that once an employee relinquishes dominion and control of a travel advance to the government, those funds again become public funds. Consequently, the government is responsible for the money.

LODGING

Travelers are entitled to reimbursement expenses for overnight sleeping facilities and certain service charges, including room taxes, when such charges are not included in the room rate.

Travelers should always stay in a "fire safe" facility. This is a facility that meets the fire safety requirements of the Hotel and Motel Fire Safety Act of 1990 as amended (5 U.S.C. 5707a).

When selecting a commercial lodging facility, first consideration must be given to government agreement programs such as FedRooms, as stated in FTR section 301-11.11.

To further assist agencies and travelers with lodging requirements, this section outlines certain lodging reimbursement entitlements and how those entitlements are determined.

107 What is FedRooms?

FedRooms is a GSA program that provides hotel rooms for federal government travelers while on official business. It is one of GSA's government-wide solutions intended to enable employees to manage their travel efficiently and effectively while accomplishing their missions. FedRooms leverages the government's buying power to offer safe, economical, and compliant hotel lodging at per diem or better rates at hotels globally. The FedRooms rate includes no early checkout fees or hidden fees. By encouraging the use of FedRooms properties and rates, agencies can ensure FTR compliance and reduce their travel spending while still meeting their missions.

108 Are travelers required to stay in lodging facilities that are part of an agency's lodging programs in addition to the GSA-sponsored FedRooms lodging program?

Yes. Agency lodging agreement programs provides leverage for government buying power. When an agency negotiates a lodging rate at specific lodging facilities that saves the government funds, travelers are required to follow agency policy. If not, they may be subject to absorbing any costs above the government-agreed rate.

In GSBCA 16384-TRAV, *In the Matter of Joel Butcher* (September 30, 2004), the Department of Agriculture (USDA) in Heber, Utah, hired several new employees in 2003. Butcher, along with other new employees, was issued blanket travel authorization to attend a new employee orientation in Salt Lake City, Utah, on February 12–14.

The authorization was issued to the employees as a group along with instructions on how to secure lodgings. Those instructions noted that employees were to make arrangements at one of the three hotels USDA had contracted with for the event before February 1. The agency emphasized that that it had procured a special lodging rate with these vendors.

Apparently, Butcher was not informed that he was required to attend the orientation until approximately a week before the event, which was past the deadline for reserving a room at a designated hotel. Assuming that rooms would no longer be available from those vendors, he did not contact them and instead arranged lodging at a hotel in Brighton, Utah. The nightly rates for that hotel were lower than those of the approved hotels. However, Brighton was farther from Salt Lake City than his PDS.

Butcher did not seek approval from his supervisor for his alternative travel and lodging plans. Also, he was the only employee to stay in a non-designated hotel. Moreover, all except one chose to commute from Heber in government vehicles.

Butcher attended the session and stayed each night in Brighton. Upon returning to his PDS, he submitted a request for reimbursement for his lodging costs but not his mileage expenses.

USDA denied the request, explaining that FTR 301-2.3 provides that "an employee traveling on official business is expected to exercise the same care in incurring expenses that a prudent person would exercise if traveling on personal business." In this situation, a prudent person on personal travel would not have elected to stay at a location farther away from the ultimate destination than the original location (residence or office). USDA believed Butcher's choices to be particularly imprudent because rooms were available at the designated hotels.

The agency also noted that it believed Butcher chose to stay in Brighton so he could meet friends to ski at night. This belief was based on comments to that effect he made to his supervisor. Given this intent, USDA concluded that his stay in Brighton was not in the government's best interest and instead served his personal activities. Butcher appealed to the GSBCA.

The board rejected the appeal. It emphasized that Butcher had never attempted to contact the designated hotels. Had he done so, he would have learned that rooms were available. In addition, he did not seek permission from his supervisor to deviate from the agency's travel instructions. Further, his alternative arrangements required him to drive farther than his colleagues who elected to commute from their PDS.

According to the board, all these facts made clear that Butcher's stay in Brighton served no mission-related purpose. Because the costs were not "necessary for or related to his temporary duty travel," they could not be reimbursed.

109 If a traveler shares a room with a co-worker, how is the lodging reimbursement calculated?

FTR section 301-11.13 states that reimbursement is "limited to one-half of the double occupancy rate if the person sharing the room is another government employee on official travel. If the person sharing the room is not a government employee on official travel, your reimbursement is limited to the single occupancy rate." You must also provide a lodging receipt regardless of the amount with your travel claim according to FTR section 301-11.25.

110 Can a traveler separate lodging taxes for foreign travel?

No. For foreign areas, lodging taxes are included in the per diem rate and cannot be separated. However, for CONUS, you may exclude the lodging taxes based only on the lodging rate paid and certain related lodging fees in accordance with FTR sections 301-11.27 and 301-12.1 in order to stay within your lodging per diem.

111 If a traveler stays with family or friends, can he/she be reimbursed the per diem rate for lodging?

Employees on travel may be reimbursed lodging costs even if they stay with relatives or friends. Reimbursement is limited, however, to the "additional cost" the friend or relative incurs in accommodating the employee rather than the maximum per diem for the area.

The traveler will not be reimbursed the cost of comparable conventional lodging in the area or a flat "token" amount but rather the additional costs the host incurs in accommodating him/her. The traveler must substantiate the costs and the traveler's agency must determine them to be reasonable.

In GSBCA 15338-TRAV, *In the Matter of Javier R. Hernandez* (October 11, 2000), an employee of the Department of Justice (DOJ) in Laredo, Texas, was authorized for an extended temporary duty assignment in Charleston, South Carolina. His travel authorization specified maximum amounts for lodging and per diem.

Hernandez's assignment lasted 148 days. Rather than renting an apartment or a hotel room, he rented the second floor of his brother's home. At the end of his assignment, Hernandez submitted a voucher for the maximum allowable per diem for lodging in the area, $13,600.

DOJ advised Hernandez that since he had stayed with his brother, he was not entitled to the maximum per diem amount. It urged him to correct the voucher and submit any evidence he had regarding the additional expense his brother incurred.

Hernandez submitted a new voucher for $5,922, claiming $43.53 per day for each day of lodging. He explained that the amount was an "average of the total cost incurred by his brother divided by 136 total days on detail." As proof of the cost, Hernandez submitted copies of his brother's federal tax return, Schedule E.

DOJ disputed the sufficiency of the evidence. In response, Hernandez submitted additional information, including his brother's receipts for utilities, phone, cable TV, towels, pillows, toiletries, carpet cleaning, furniture, sheets, and appliances.

DOJ denied the second revised voucher, informing Hernandez that the documentation did not "substantiate additional out-of-pocket expenses" incurred by his brother. Hernandez appealed to the GSBCA. He argued that the FTR, section 301-11.15, allows travelers to be paid the following expenses when renting a room on a long-term basis: (1) the rental cost of a furnished dwelling; (2) if unfurnished, the rental cost of the dwelling and the cost of appropriate and necessary furniture and appliances; (3) the cost of connecting and disconnecting utilities; (4) the cost of reasonable maid fees; (5) the cost of monthly telephone use; and (6) if ordinarily included in the price of a hotel room, the cost of special user fees.

The board was not persuaded, believing that Hernandez's reliance on FTR 301-11.15 was misplaced. The provision deals with either a landlord's charges to a traveler or costs incurred directly by a traveler resulting from a long-term stay. It does not address reimbursement for costs incurred by a relative running his household.

The board stated that the applicable FTR section was 301-11.12(c). That section provides that travelers who stay with friends or relatives "may be reimbursed the additional costs their hosts incur in accommodating them only if they are able to substantiate the costs and their agency determines the expenses are reasonable." Travelers are not entitled to the cost of conventional lodging in the area or a flat "token" amount.

According to the board, Hernandez was seeking his brother's household maintenance costs rather than additional expenses his brother had incurred. For example, Hernandez requested reimbursement for the full cost of an entertainment system, furniture, lawn care equipment, mattresses, and plumbing supplies. These items had a useful life far beyond Hernandez's stay. Moreover, they benefited his entire family and not just Hernandez. As a result, DOJ should not be responsible for their cost.

While the costs of consumables and utility services are generally reimbursable, the board found that DOJ should not pay them in this case. Agencies are responsible only for the portion of such items and services used by a government employee. Hernandez failed to submit sufficient receipts to make that determination. Therefore, the board concluded that DOJ should not reimburse any of the requested amount.

112 Are there any situations when a traveler can be reimbursed for lodging expenses when staying with a relative or friend?

The purpose of the rule, as discussed in question #111, is to ensure that while the government reimburses costs of lodging that are incurred through a business relationship, it does not promote arrangements made between closely aligned individuals for the purpose of enriching the employee, the host, or both. However, if the friend or relative is in the business of operating a hotel or apartment house, the "friends or relatives" provision of the FTR does not apply.

113 If an agency has a remote location for employees performing TDY and there is no hotel within a reasonable driving distance, can employees use their own RV and be reimbursed a daily amount?

FTR section 301-11.12 states in part that "Your agency will reimburse you for nonconventional lodging when there are no conventional lodging facilities in the area (e.g., in remote areas). . . you may be reimbursed for expenses (parking fees, fees for connection, use, and disconnection of utilities, electricity, gas, water and sewage, bath or shower fees, and dumping fees) which may be considered as a lodging cost" for a recreational vehicle (trailer/camper).

TRANSPORTATION

Agencies are required to reimburse travelers the full cost of transportation for authorized travel between the employee's PDS or other authorized departure point and the TDY site and return. Agencies are also required to pay certain transportation expenses that the employee incurs while at the TDY site.

As a traveler, you must travel to your destination by the usually traveled route unless your agency authorizes or approves a different route as officially necessary. If, for personal convenience, you travel by an indirect route or interrupt travel by a direct route, your reimbursement will be limited to the cost of travel by a direct route or on an uninterrupted basis. You will be responsible for any additional costs. Your agency must select the method of transportation most advantageous to the government when considering cost and other factors. (See Approving Official Responsibilities in *Part IV, Before You Travel.*)

Travel by common carrier is presumed to be the most advantageous method of transportation and must be used when reasonably available. When your agency determines that your travel must be performed by automobile, a government automobile is presumed to be the most advantageous method of transportation.

This section provides basic information on incurring and reimbursement of expenses related to the most common modes of transportation. For a mode of transportation not addressed, consult with your agency travel manager.

Airline Expenses

Transportation by common carrier (commercial) air is generally the most cost-efficient and expeditious way to travel. However, certain expenses related to commercial air travel may be restricted or limited, depending on the situation. The traveler should be aware of the requirements for traveling by common carrier air to avoid financial liability for unauthorized expenses.

114 Can an agency reimburse a traveler for purchasing an airline ticket from an unauthorized source?

Agencies are required to reimburse travelers for the cost of purchasing airfare from an unauthorized travel agent up to the total amount a ticket would have cost had it been purchased from an authorized source. However, agencies may take disciplinary action against employees who do not follow agency travel policy.

In GSBCA 15692-TRAV, *In the Matter of D. Gregory Arnold* (January 18, 2000), a civilian employee of the Department of the Air Force in Ohio was authorized to attend a Defense Acquisition

University class in Florida. He enrolled in the class and arranged for his family to accompany him on the trip.

Arnold's airline ticket was purchased through a commercial travel office (CTO) selected by the Air Force, at a cost of $208. Unfortunately, a week before the class began, Arnold learned that due to an administrative error, he had been placed on the waiting list for the class rather than enrolled in it. His supervisor suggested that he proceed with his plans to travel to Florida with his family, pay for his own airline ticket, and appear for the first meeting of the class. The supervisor further advised him that if he was successful in enrolling for the two-week course, travel orders for his attendance would be issued after he returned. If he was unable to enroll, he should simply remain with his family in Florida and the time would be charged to his annual leave.

Arnold followed his supervisor's advice. He canceled his ticket, which had been purchased through the CTO, and instead purchased different airfare at a cost of $202. Upon arriving in Florida, he was able to successfully enroll in the class.

The Air Force issued confirming travel orders on his return. In addition, it reimbursed him all his TDY assignment costs except the $202 he spent on airfare. It informed him that since he did not buy the ticket from a CTO, in-house travel office, or General Services Travel Management Center as required by subparagraph C2207-A.1 of the JTR, he was not entitled to reimbursement for that expense.

Arnold appealed to the GSBCA, which found he was entitled to reimbursement.

The board emphasized that Section 301-50.2 of the FTR, which is binding on all defense agencies in addition to the JTR, requires agencies to reimburse employees for the cost of purchasing airfare from an unauthorized travel agent, up to the total a ticket would have cost had it been purchased from an authorized source. Because Arnold's original ticket purchased through the CTO cost $208 and the ticket he purchased cost $202, he was entitled to reimbursement for the full amount. If the cost of the ticket had exceeded the total of the CTO-purchased airfare, his reimbursement would have been capped at $208.

In issuing the decision, the GSBCA noted that it has decided multiple cases over the past few years with similar circumstances. As a result, it encouraged Air Force senior officials to remind all agency travel and finance offices of this rule so that "in the future, claims will be resolved with Board decisions in mind, thereby avoiding futile defenses of repetitious cases."

115 Are there any circumstances under which a traveler can be reimbursed for the total cost of an airline ticket purchased from an unauthorized source?

The GSBCA issued a decision in 2000 in which it determined that an unusual circumstance allowed a traveler to be reimbursed for the total cost of an airline ticket purchased from an unauthorized source.

In GSBCA 15197-TRAV, *In the Matter of In the Matter of Robert E. Dawes* (February 1, 2000), an employee of the Department of the Air Force based in California was scheduled to attend a conference in Colorado. Ten days before the trip, Dawes purchased round-trip airline tickets from his agency's designated CTO. When he arrived at the airport and checked in at the gate 30 minutes before the scheduled flight, Dawes realized that he had forgotten his tickets. Since there was not enough time to return home and get the tickets, Dawes purchased replacement tickets directly from the airline. He did not want to take a later flight because he had arranged for a conference coordinator to meet him at the airport in Colorado and he had no way of contacting her to inform her of a change in flight plans.

When Dawes returned to California, he was able to return the unused tickets to the CTO for a full refund. When he requested reimbursement from the Air Force for the replacement tickets he had purchased, his claim was denied. The Air Force contended that Dawes was not entitled to reimbursement because he failed to purchase the tickets from the CTO.

The GSBCA rejected the Air Force's reasoning. In determining whether an employee has an alternative, the board recognized that the alternative must be a reasonable one. An employee is not required to exercise an alternative, however unreasonable, merely because it exists. Rather, the employee is entitled to use his/her judgment in assessing the reasonableness of the alternative in light of specific factual conditions.

Dawes had no alternative but to purchase replacement tickets directly from the airline when he realized he had forgotten the tickets only 30 minutes before his scheduled flight. Although the board noted that Dawes conceivably could have tried calling the CTO to see if it could arrange new tickets in time for him to make his flight, this was an unlikely possibility and was therefore not a reasonable alternative.

Further, although he could have canceled the trip, this decision would have resulted in a delay in his TDY assignment and would have caused inconvenience for the colleague he had arranged to meet in Colorado. Thus, this option was not a reasonable alternative either under the circumstances. Since Dawes' decision to purchase replacement tickets was reasonable in light of the various factors he was forced to confront, his use of a non-contract agent fell within the "unusual circumstances" exception and he was entitled to reimbursement.

116 Can a traveler be reimbursed for flight insurance?

No, federal travelers may not be reimbursed for flight insurance. The purchase of flight or accident insurance is considered a personal expense and therefore is not reimbursable (FTR section 301-10.452). Likewise, trip cancellation insurance is not reimbursable.

117 Are contractors allowed to use contract city pair fares to perform travel under their contracts?

No. If an agency has established a centrally billed account (CBA) to track travel expenses for contractors, it should have a separate CBA account numbering structure that denotes no access to the airline city pair fares. Further, contractors are not considered invitational travelers and should not share a CBA with such orders.

118 If a traveler's city has more than one airport, can the traveler's supervisor require that he/she use a specific airport for TDY travel?

Yes. Although you may generally use any airport that best suits your needs (for example, one that is closer to your residence than to your PDS), your supervisor has the authority to direct the use of a specific airport in accordance with agency policy. Cities that have multiple airports include Chicago, Dallas/Ft. Worth, Detroit, Houston, Los Angeles, New York, San Francisco, and Washington, D.C.

119 When can an agency authorize a rest period?

An agency may authorize a rest period not in excess of 24 hours at either an intermediate point or at the traveler's destination if:

- Either the origin or destination point is OCONUS
- The traveler's scheduled flight time, including stopovers, exceeds 14 hours
- Travel is by a direct or usually traveled route
- Travel is by coach-class service.

When a rest stop is authorized, the applicable per diem rate is the rate for the rest stop location.

120 For flight time over 14 hours, can a traveler request premium class accommodations instead of a rest period?

Travelers do not make the decision or determine how they may travel, including use of premium class accommodations. Federal employees must travel as directed by their agency. A traveler is not entitled to premium-class accommodations just because the flight time is more than 14 hours. FTR section 301-70.100 requires agencies to "limit authorization and payment of transportation expenses to those expenses that result in the greatest advantage to the government."

Therefore, the agency has discretion to authorize either accommodations other than coach class in accordance with FTR section 301-10.125 or a rest period in accordance with FTR section 301-11.20.

121 When can a traveler upgrade an airline ticket above coach-class accommodations?

Although the government normally requires travelers to fly in coach class, a traveler can choose to upgrade class accommodations at his/her own expense, including using personal frequent-flyer miles earned previously on official trips. Once the official ticket has been issued reflecting the coach-class accommodations, the traveler may then exchange the ticket to accommodate the upgrade request.

Since an upgrade is a contract between the traveler and the airline, the traveler is responsible for any fees or penalties associated with the upgrade. However, an agency may reimburse a traveler for an upgraded ticket to accommodate a special physical need if the upgrade is authorized and priority seating is guaranteed. See also Special Needs in *Part IV: Before You Travel* and questions #123 and #124.

122 What are the classes of accommodations for air travel?

Airlines are constantly updating their offerings. Generally, the classes of available air accommodations are identified and defined as follows:

- *Coach class* – The basic class of accommodation that is normally the lowest fare offered. Airlines sometimes refer to coach class as tourist class, economy class, or single class when they offer only one class of accommodations to all travelers.
- *Other than coach class* – Any class of accommodations above coach class. This includes first class, which is the highest class of accommodation offered by the airlines in terms of cost and amenities, and business class, which is higher than coach class and lower than first class in both cost and amenities. Different airlines refer to business class as business elite, business first, world business, connoisseur, or envoy.

If an airline flight has only two classes of accommodations available (i.e., two "cabins"), with two distinctly different seating types (such as girth and pitch), and the front cabin is termed business class or higher by the airline and the tickets are fare-coded as business class, then the front of the cabin is deemed to be other than coach class. Alternatively, if an airline flight has only two cabins available but equips both with one type of seating (i.e., seating girth and pitch are the same in both cabins), the seats in the front of the airplane are coded as full-fare economy class, and only restricted economy fares are available in the back of the aircraft, then the entire aircraft is classified as coach-class seating. In this second situation, qualifying for other-than-coach-class travel is not required to purchase a non-restricted economy fare seat in the front of the aircraft because the entire aircraft is considered coach class.

123 When may a traveler fly first class?

Government travelers are required to exercise the same care in incurring expenses that a prudent person would exercise if traveling on personal business when making official travel arrangements; accordingly, government travelers should consider the least expensive class of travel that meets their needs. First-class accommodations may be used only when the agency specifically authorizes this use under the following circumstances:

- No coach-class accommodations are reasonably available. "Reasonably available" means available on an airline that is scheduled to leave within 24 hours of your proposed departure time or scheduled to arrive within 24 hours of your proposed arrival time.
- Use of other than coach class is necessary to accommodate a medical disability or other special need, including an attendant to accompany you.
- Exceptional security circumstances require other-than-coach-class airline accommodations. Exceptional security circumstances are determined by your agency and should be authorized only up to the minimum that other-than-coach-class accommodations are necessary. These circumstances include, but are not limited to:

  - Use of coach-class accommodations would endanger your life or government property
  - You are an agent on protective detail and you are accompanying an individual authorized to use other-than-coach-class accommodations
  - You are a courier or control officer accompanying controlled pouches or packages.

124 When may an agency authorize/approve business-class accommodations?

An agency may authorize/approve business-class accommodations if any of the following apply:

- Use of other than coach class is necessary to accommodate a medical disability or other special need.
- Exceptional security circumstances require other-than-coach-class airline accommodations. Exceptional security circumstances are determined by your agency and should be authorized only to the minimum that other-than-coach-class accommodations are necessary to meet the agency's mission. These circumstances include, but are not limited to:
  - Use of coach-class accommodations would endanger your life or government property
  - You are an agent on protective detail and you are accompanying an individual authorized to use other-than-coach-class accommodations
  - You are a courier or control officer accompanying controlled pouches or packages.

125 What documentation is required to travel first class or business class if a traveler has a medical disability?

A disability must be certified annually in a written statement by a competent medical authority. However, if the disability is a lifelong condition, then a one-time certification statement is required. Certification statements must include at a minimum:

- Written statement by a competent medical authority stating that special accommodation is necessary
- Approximate duration of the special accommodation
- Recommendation regarding the suitable class of transportation accommodations based on the disability.

126 What documentation is required to travel first class or business class if a traveler has a special need?

A special need must be certified annually in writing according to the agency's procedures. However, if the special need is a lifelong condition, then a one-time certification statement is required. If you are authorized additional travel expenses as an employee with special needs to have an attendant accompany you, your agency may also authorize the attendant to use other-than-coach-class accommodations if you require the attendant's services en route.

127 What other exceptions are acceptable to travel in first-class or business-class accommodations?

An agency may authorize or approve first-class or business-class accommodations in any of the following circumstances:

- Coach-class accommodations on an authorized/approved foreign air carrier do not provide adequate sanitation or health standards
- Regularly scheduled flights between origin/destination points (including connecting points) provide only other-than-coach-class accommodations and you certify such on your voucher
- The traveler's transportation costs are paid in full through agency acceptance of payment from a non-federal source in accordance with the FTR
- The origin or destination are OCONUS and the scheduled flight time, including stopovers and change of planes, is in excess of 14 hours

- Overall cost savings to the government is achieved by avoiding additional subsistence costs, overtime, or lost productive time while awaiting coach-class accommodations
- No space is available in coach-class accommodations in time to accomplish the mission, which is urgent and cannot be postponed
- Such accommodations are required based on agency mission, consistent with the agency's internal procedures in accordance with the FTR.

128 Can other-than-coach-class accommodations be authorized for travel on a foreign carrier?

Other-than-coach-class accommodations may also be authorized on a foreign carrier if:

- The foreign air carrier does not provide adequate sanitation or health standards in coach class
- Regularly scheduled flights between origin/destination points (including connecting points) provide only other-than-coach-class accommodations and you certify such on your voucher
- Your transportation costs are paid in full through agency acceptance of payment from a non-federal source in accordance with established policies and procedures
- The origin or destination is OCONUS and the scheduled flight time, including stopovers and change of planes, is in excess of 14 hours
- Overall cost to the government is reduced by avoiding additional subsistence costs, overtime, or lost productive time while awaiting coach-class accommodations
- No space is available in coach-class accommodations in time to accomplish the mission, which is urgent and cannot be postponed.

A traveler may, however, upgrade to other-than-coach-class accommodations at personal expense, including through redemption of frequent-flyer benefits.

129 Can blanket authorization be used for other-than-coach class accommodations?

In general, blanket authorization of other-than-coach-class transportation accommodations is prohibited. Such accommodations must be authorized on an individual trip-by-trip basis, unless the traveler has an up-to-date documented disability or special need.

Fly America Act

The Fly America Act requires that foreign air travel funded with federal dollars be performed on U.S. flag air carriers, unless a traveler meets one of the act's strict exceptions.

130 What does "U.S. flag air carrier" mean?

A U.S. flag air carrier is an air carrier that holds a certificate issued by the United States under 49 U.S.C. 41102; foreign carriers operating under a permit are not included.

131 What is a code-share agreement?

A code-share agreement is a marketing arrangement where one airline puts its code on the flights of another airline in order to coordinate services and advertise and sell the other airline's services as its own (i.e., the code-share flights are marketed by U.S. carriers as their own flights). Some or all of the transportation is provided by another carrier, which carries its partner's designator code. Code-share agreements are common practice.

132 What information is required from a traveler when a foreign carrier is used?

When using a foreign air carrier, a traveler will need to provide a certification regarding why a foreign air carrier must be used. According to FTR section 301-10.142, the certification must include the traveler's name; the dates of travel; the origin and destination of travel; a detailed itinerary of the travel, including the name of the air carrier and flight number for each leg of the trip; and a statement explaining how the travel meets one of the exceptions to the requirements of the Fly America Act.

133 What exceptions to the Fly America Act requirements apply when travel is between the United States and another country?

If a U.S. flag air carrier offers nonstop or direct service (no aircraft change) from your origin to your destination, you must use the U.S. flag air carrier service unless such use would extend your travel time, including delay at origin, by 24 hours or more.

If a U.S. flag air carrier does not offer nonstop or direct service between your origin and your destination, you must use a U.S. flag air carrier on every portion of the route where it provides service unless, when compared to using a foreign air carrier, such use would result in one of the following:

- Increase the number of aircraft changes you must make outside the United States by two or more
- Extend your travel time by six hours or more
- Require a connecting time of four hours or more at an overseas interchange point.

134 What exceptions to the Fly America Act requirements apply when travel is solely outside the United States and a U.S. flag air carrier provides service between the traveler's origin and destination?

A traveler must always use a U.S. flag carrier for such travel unless, when compared to using a foreign air carrier, such use would:

- Increase the number of aircraft changes you must make outside the United States by two or more
- Extend your travel time by six hours or more

- Require a connecting time of four hours or more at an overseas interchange point.

135 May a traveler use a foreign air carrier if the service is preferred by or more convenient for the traveler or his/her agency?

No. The traveler must use U.S. flag air carrier service unless the traveler meets one of the exceptions as stated above or unless foreign air carrier service is deemed a matter of necessity.

136 Is reliance on the judgment of an official travel agent a defense to violating the Fly America Act?

No. As the following GSBCA decision demonstrates, federal employees are "responsible for performing official travel correctly . . . and for the payment of any charges incurred through failure to comply with governing regulations, regardless of who may have assisted the traveler in making the travel arrangements."

In GSBCA 15012-TRAV, *In the Matter of Desiree Fray* (July 23, 1999), a Department of State (DOS) employee at the U.S. Consulate General in Cape Town, South Africa, was authorized to travel round trip from Cape Town to Washington, D.C. DOS's travel agent booked Fray on American Airlines from Cape Town to Miami, Florida, and from Miami to Washington, D.C. For her return trip, the travel agent booked Fray through Europe since flights to Cape Town through Miami were not available on the day Fray wanted to travel. The agent booked Fray on United Airlines from Washington to London and on South African Airways from London to Cape Town.

The untaxed price of Fray's ticket was 12,610 South African rands. The fares for a direct return to Cape Town through Miami on American Airlines and for a return to Cape Town through London on United Airlines and South African Airways were the same. As a result, the travel agent assumed that booking the last leg of the trip on a foreign carrier was acceptable.

Upon returning, Fray submitted a travel voucher totaling $2,318.48 for all her expenses, excluding airfare. Fray had already received a travel advance of $2,247. Consequently, she expected to receive a check for $71.48. Instead, DOS claimed that she had violated the Fly America Act by using South African Airways and therefore owed the government $1,286.40.

DOS explained that the penalty for not flying a U.S.-flagged carrier was $1,357.88—the cost of Fray's ticket from London to Cape Town. In reaching the final figure of 1,286.40, DOS simply subtracted the $71.48 it owed Fray for outstanding travel expenses from the penalty for violating the Fly America Act.

Fray appealed to the GSBCA. She argued that she should not be assessed the penalty because she had only followed the advice of her travel agent.

The GSBCA was not persuaded. The board noted that the Fly America Act requires federal employees to use U.S.-flagged vessels for flights within and from the United States, unless "use of a foreign carrier is necessary." The board has interpreted "necessary" as including medical emergencies or if no seats are available on a U.S. carrier.

In this situation, seats were available. Moreover, it did not matter that Fray relied on the judgment of DOS's travel agent. According to the board, all federal employees are "responsible for performing official travel correctly . . . and for the payment of any charges incurred through failure to comply with governing regulations, regardless of who may have assisted the traveler in making the travel arrangements."

137 May an employee travel by a foreign air carrier if the cost of the ticket is less than traveling by a U.S. flag air carrier?

No. Foreign air carrier service may not be used solely based on the cost of the ticket.

138 Is a traveler required to provide any special certification or documents if he/she uses a foreign air carrier?

Yes. The traveler must provide certification and any other documents required by the traveler's agency.

139 What must the certification for using a foreign air carrier include?

The certification must include:

- The traveler's name
- The dates of travel
- The origin and the destination of the travel
- A detailed itinerary of the travel, name of the air carrier, and flight number of each leg of the trip
- A statement explaining why the traveler met one of the exceptions in accordance with FTR section 301-10.135, 301-10.136, or 301-10.137, or a copy of the traveler's agency's written approval that foreign air carrier service was deemed a matter of necessity in accordance with FTR section 301-10.138.

Your agency may not pay your foreign air carrier fare if you do not provide the required certification.

140 If a traveler does not meet the exceptions for using a foreign carrier but learns that the foreign carrier is also a code-share partner with a U.S. flag carrier, can the traveler be reimbursed for the airline ticket?

No. Air travel paid by the federal government must occur on U.S. flag carriers wherever possible. The government may make exceptions to this rule only when the traveler proves that the use of a foreign air carrier was necessary.

In CBCA 1625-RELO, *In the Matter of Token D. Barnthouse,* (January 8, 2010), a Navy civilian employee was relocated from a naval base in Guam to Sigonella, Italy, in July 2008. While traveling to Italy, he missed his connecting flight in Los Angeles. The events that occurred next became the subject of a dispute between Barnthouse and the Navy.

Barnthouse, believing that his original tickets from Los Angeles to Italy became "null and void" when he missed his connecting flight, bought another set of tickets from another carrier, Alitalia Airlines. On his new itinerary, he traveled from Los Angeles International Airport (LAX) to Rome ($2,442.16) and from Rome to Catania, Italy ($400). Barnthouse paid the total balance with a personal credit card.

Barnthouse submitted a voucher for reimbursement of the alternate route. The Navy paid him $400 for the flight from Rome to Catania because no American carrier operates on this route. However, the Navy rejected his costs for travel from LAX to Rome on the basis that he was required to travel on an airline based in the United States. Barnthouse, noting that he had seen other U.S. military members traveling on the same Alitalia flight to Rome, appealed to the CBCA for reimbursement of the remaining $2,442.16.

The Navy told the CBCA that it didn't understand why Barnthouse had missed his connecting flight in the first place. He had been scheduled to arrive at LAX at 5:00 a.m. on a Continental Airlines flight and depart LAX at 7:15 a.m. on an American Airlines flight to Chicago, Illinois; the Navy confirmed that both flights had been on time. The Navy's representative stated: "This gave [Barnthouse] approximately two hours to get from one flight to the other. [His] claim that the ticket was void because he did not have time to connect to the flight seems unlikely unless there are other mitigating circumstances that [he] has not mentioned."

The Navy also asserted that it could not reimburse travel via a foreign flag air carrier when a route was available through a U.S.-based air carrier. It explained that Barnthouse may have seen other military members on the same flight under official travel, but their tickets had been purchased from a U.S. air carrier: "U.S. flag carriers routinely use foreign flag carriers to transport their customers with connecting flights including military members. When the airlines and the government do this, these travelers, while using the assigned foreign flag carrier, are traveling under an American airline flight number thus staying in the parameters of using an American airline."

Last, the Navy noted that Barnthouse had not provided sufficient detail on his purchases: "The only proof of purchase he provided was a credit card statement from Navy Federal Credit Union showing a purchase was made from Alitalia Airlines on July 31, 2008. He has not provided an itinerary from the flight nor an itemized breakdown of what the expenses were. For all we know he purchased a first class ticket, multiple tickets, or paid pet transportation fees which are unauthorized for travel at government expense."

The CBCA agreed that each of the Navy's reasons for rejecting reimbursement was valid. Under the Fly America Act, 49 U.S.C. 40118(a)(3)(B) (2006), air travel paid by the federal government must occur on U.S. flag carriers wherever possible. The government may make exceptions to this rule only when the traveler proves that the use of a foreign air carrier was necessary. This statute is reflected in JTR C2204-C.2. Accordingly, the CBCA rejected Barnthouse's claim.

Open Skies

Open Skies is an agreement that allows certain foreign nations' airlines the right to transport passengers and cargo on scheduled or charter flights for U.S. government–procured transportation. These agreements do not apply to the DoD Uniformed Services nor to DoD civilian employees unless their travel is funded by a non-DoD agency in accordance with that agency's/service's policy if a city-pair flight is not available for the scheduled official travel between the origin and destination.

141 When can a traveler use Open Skies?

If authorized by the agency, a traveler may use Open Skies if the traveler meets the exceptions under the Fly America Act to use a foreign carrier as stated in questions #133 and #134. The traveler cannot use transportation service under Open Skies if the transportation is between points for which there is a city-pair contract fare in effect for air passenger transportation services or the transportation is obtained or funded by the Secretary of Defense or the Secretary of a military department.

142 What are the exceptions for Open Skies?

The exceptions are:

- If a U.S. flag air carrier offers nonstop or direct service (no aircraft change) from your origin to your destination, you must use the U.S. flag air carrier service unless such use would extend your travel time, including delay at origin, by 24 hours or more.
- If a U.S. flag air carrier does not offer nonstop or direct service between your origin and your destination, you must use a U.S. flag air carrier on every portion of the route where it provides service unless, when compared to using a foreign air carrier, such use would:
  - Increase the number of aircraft changes you must make outside the United States by two or more
  - Extend your travel time by six hours or more
  - Require a connecting time of four hours or more at an overseas interchange point.

Train Expenses

The rules governing the class of service for rail transportation are the same as the rules governing common-air-carrier class of service. Travelers should generally travel by coach-class train service.

143 What's an extra-fare train?

An extra-fare train is a train that operates at an increased fare based on the extra performance of the train (e.g., faster speed or fewer stops such as the Acela and Metroliner).

144 When can a traveler use an extra-fare train?

A traveler may use extra-fare train service when the agency determines that doing so is more advantageous to the government or is required for security reasons. Extra-fare train service is considered to be a class above the lowest class offered on any particular train and must be authorized/approved as required for accommodations above coach class.

145 When can a traveler use train accommodations above coach class?

A traveler may use other-than-coach-class accommodations only when the agency specifically authorizes such use under the same circumstances as for air travel as discussed in questions #123 through #127.

146 If the approving official authorizes train transportation for an employee's TDY, can the employee choose to drive a POV instead?

FTR section 301-10.4 requires an approving official to select the method of transportation most advantageous to the government when cost and other factors are considered. However, FTR section 301-70.105 states in part that the approving official may not prohibit an employee from using his/her POV but must limit reimbursement to the "constructive cost of the authorized method of transportation . . . [and the employee must] charge leave for any duty hours that are missed as a result of travel by POV."

POV Expenses

Use of a POV may be authorized when determined advantageous to the government. However, travelers cannot receive reimbursement for additional days of travel incurred as a result of choosing to travel by POV. In all cases, using a POV to transport other employees is strictly voluntary.

147 If co-workers travel together in a POV and share the driving expenses, can they both claim per diem expenses?

In accordance with FTR section 301-10.305, "If another employee(s) travels with you on the same trip in the same POV, mileage is payable to only one of you. No deduction will be made from your mileage allowance if other passengers contribute to defraying your expenses."

148 If use of a POV results in additional travel time, can the traveler be reimbursed per diem for the extra days?

Reimbursement for extra travel days depends on the result of a constructive cost analysis performed by your agency. The constructive cost analysis is based on the authorized method of common-carrier transportation plus per diem.

149 If an employee's driver's license is suspended but will be reinstated prior to an upcoming TDY assignment, can the traveler still be authorized to drive a government vehicle?

In accordance with FTR section 310.10-220, "You must possess a valid State, District of Columbia or territorial motor vehicle operator's license and have a travel authorization specifically authorizing the use of a government-furnished automobile." Therefore, it is reasonable to assume that a traveler must meet the requirement for driving a government vehicle at the time the travel authorization is prepared. Also, if travel is a requirement in the performance of the employee's official duties, withholding such information may be viewed as a violation of standards of conduct.

150 If a traveler is authorized to use a government-owned automobile but uses a POV instead, how is reimbursement calculated?

The traveler will be reimbursed based on a constructive mileage rate, which is limited to the cost that would be incurred for use of a government automobile (GOA). If the agency determines that the cost of providing a GOA would be higher because of unusual circumstances, it may allow reimbursement not to exceed the mileage rate for a POV. In addition, the traveler may be reimbursed other allowable mileage expenses, such as tolls and parking, as authorized by the agency and in accordance with the FTR.

In GSBCA 15231-TRAV, *In the Matter of Charles M. Auker* (April 24, 2000), a civilian employee of DoD in Cuyahoga, Ohio, was assigned to the Defense Contract Management Command (DCMC) in Akron, Ohio. In July, Auker was directed to report to an office in Bratenahl, Ohio, for a meeting and to obtain safety shoes from a store in Cleveland, Ohio. DoD did not state what means of transportation Auker should use. Without seeking authorization to use a POV, Auker drove his own car to the meeting in Bratenahl and to obtain safety shoes in Cleveland. The trip totaled 82 miles.

Auker submitted a reimbursement voucher for 31 cents per mile. DoD refused to reimburse him at the maximum POV rate and instead reimbursed him at 10.5 cents per mile. DoD informed Auker that it had not authorized him to use a POV, noting that he should have used one of the four government-owned vehicles the agency maintains in Akron.

Auker appealed to the GSBCA. He claimed that he had not been permitted to use a government-owned vehicle on a previous trip and had instead been authorized to use his own car. As a result, he had no reason to believe he would be authorized to use a government-owned vehicle for this trip.

The board was not persuaded. It emphasized that the JTR limits mileage reimbursement to 10.5 cents per mile if a government vehicle is available and the employee instead chooses to use a POV.

In this case, a government-owned vehicle was available. Auker's belief that a government vehicle would not be available since one was not for his last trip lacked any basis, according to the board. Auker should have sought authorization to use a POV. His failure to do so placed him at risk that he would be reimbursed at the lowest possible rate.

151 What does the mileage rate cover?

The mileage rate covers all costs of operating a POV, including gasoline, depreciation, insurance, and repairs. The following is a partial listing of reimbursable and non-reimbursable expenses:

Reimbursable expenses in addition to mileage allowance	Non-reimbursable expenses included in the mileage allowance
Parking fees; ferry fees; bridge, road, and tunnel fees; and aircraft or airplane parking, landing, and tie-down fees	Charges for repairs, depreciation, replacements, grease, oil, antifreeze, towage and similar speculative expenses, gasoline, insurance, state and federal taxes

152 Can a traveler be denied use of a POV if required to travel by air or if doing so is not advantageous to the government?

No, a traveler cannot be denied use of a POV instead of air travel. However, the traveler's reimbursement will be limited to the cost of travel by a direct route or on an uninterrupted basis. Any additional costs incurred for traveling an indirect route (such as an unofficial stop or a stopover for personal reasons) will be the responsibility of the traveler.

In GSBCA 14966-TRAV, *In the Matter of Bernhard Reeves* (December 6, 1999), a civilian employee of the Navy in Charleston, South Carolina, was issued travel orders to report to Norfolk, Virginia, on a TDY assignment. The TDY was scheduled to begin on February 16 and end on February 19. Reeves' travel orders authorized him to travel by air; he elected to use his own car instead.

Reeves departed from Charleston on February 14 and arrived in Norfolk on February 15. He started his TDY on February 16 and completed it on February 19 at 2:00 p.m. Immediately after completing the TDY, Reeves left Norfolk and traveled more than five hours to Havelock, North Carolina. He stayed in Havelock overnight and completed the trip the next day.

After returning, Reeves submitted a travel voucher. He requested reimbursement for February 16 through 20, including hotel expenses, full-day per diem for Friday, February 19, and three-quarters per diem for Saturday, February 20.

The Navy agreed to reimburse Reeves' full per diem for February 16 through February 18. It refused, however, to reimburse him his lodging expenses for February 19. Instead, it authorized three-quarters per diem for that day. Finally, it refused to authorize any per diem for February 20. The Navy informed Reeves that if he had traveled by air, he would have arrived home on February 19 and would not have incurred additional lodging expenses or any additional travel expenses on February 20.

Reeves appealed to the GSBCA. He argued that he should be reimbursed for a full day of per diem and lodging on his departure day and a partial per diem for the following day, to cover expenses he incurred to avoid traveling during off-duty hours.

The board rejected his appeal, noting that an employee on official travel is not ordinarily required to travel during unreasonable hours at night. If Reeves had traveled by air, he would have departed Norfolk on February 19 at 2:00 p.m., arrived in Charleston at 5:00 p.m., and arrived home from the airport at 6:30 p.m. None of these times represent unreasonable "nighttime" travel.

Since Reeves traveled by car, he took the risk that he would be forced to travel additional hours at night as well as on subsequent days. The test for reimbursement is the schedule that he would have kept had he traveled by air and not the schedule he maintained as a result of choosing to travel by POV.

Rental Car Expenses

Agencies may authorize the use of a rental car when such use is determined to be advantageous to the government. An agency must specifically authorize use of a rental car in advance of travel and must annotate the use on the traveler's travel authorization.

153 Can a traveler be reimbursed for insurance while renting a car for official travel?

No. If a traveler is authorized by his/her agency to rent a car in accordance with FTR sections 301-2.5 and 301-10.450, the traveler must decline the cost of collision damage or theft insurance coverage.

For vehicles rented for official business while in CONUS, the government is self-insured through contracts negotiated through the Defense Travel Management Office. However, the agency may reimburse the traveler for such insurance for OCONUS travel if the insurance is necessary because of rental or agency requirements or foreign laws, or because legal procedures could cause extreme difficulty for the traveler if involved an accident (FTR section 301-10.451).

154 Can a traveler be denied reimbursement for a rental car even though the expense was approved and authorized on the travel authorization?

Yes. Should the government later determine that the use of a rental car was not more advantageous to the government than some other means of transportation as stated in the FTR, the traveler may not be reimbursed for the rental car expenses.

In GSBCA 15042- TRAV, *In the Matter of Gregory E. Fife* (September 14, 1999), an employee of the Environmental Protection Agency (EPA) in Dallas, Texas, was authorized to travel to San Francisco, California, for a conference. Fife learned from a fellow EPA employee during a conference call that employees of the Bay Area Rapid Transit (BART) were planning a strike during the time of his trip and that travelers should therefore expect to pay three to four times the normal rates for taxis. Fife noted this situation when discussing with his supervisor how he would reach his hotel from the airport. There was no bus service from the airport, and the hotel did not have a shuttle. To avoid exorbitant taxi fares, Fife's supervisor authorized a rental car. Fife's travel orders were amended to reflect the change.

Upon arriving in San Francisco, Fife rented a car and, together with another EPA employee attending the meeting, drove to the hotel from the airport. Fife parked the car in the hotel garage for the duration of his stay. He used the car several times to go out to dinner and lunch and to drive back to the airport for his return flight.

The total cost of renting and parking the car was $189.23. When Fife submitted a voucher for reimbursement, EPA refused to pay the full cost. It informed him that the rental car was not justified because commercial transportation would have been more advantageous to the government. Instead, the agency reimbursed him $60—the projected cost of using taxis (based on the $20 per ten miles charged by Dallas taxis). Fife resubmitted his claim together with documentation that taxi fare from the San Francisco airport to downtown is approximately $30–35.

EPA again denied the claim. However, it raised the reimbursement amount to $140, reasoning that because Fife had provided a colleague transportation from the airport, he was entitled to the cost of a two-passenger taxi fare rather than a solo fare.

Fife appealed to the GSBCA. The board denied his appeal, noting that, generally, "travel orders which authorize the use of a rental car are deemed to be in error unless the facts clearly establish that the car was advantageous to the government or was used for official business." In this case, the facts did not clearly indicate that renting a car would have been cheaper than using local public transportation.

The board emphasized that the source of Fife's claim that taxi fares would be excessive was based solely on a remark made by another employee during a conference call. On arriving in San Francisco, Fife made no effort to verify a rate hike. In addition, EPA was unable to independently verify that taxi fares had increased. An EPA certifying official called Fife's hotel to determine if hotel staff had heard guests complain of being charged excessive taxi fares, but no complaints had been reported.

Although the board recognized that Fife's travel orders permitted him to rent a car, it determined that his unconditional reliance on the document was misplaced. The authorization was predicated on the assumption that taxis or other forms of transportation might require an expenditure in excess of what would be required to rent a vehicle. Given the uncertainty of all these assumptions, the board determined that it was unreasonable for Fife to have rented the car and expected reimbursement.

155 Can a traveler be reimbursed for including a global positioning system (GPS) in the cost of the car rental?

Although no specific rule in the FTR specifically addresses the use and reimbursement of a GPS, agencies have discretion for authorizing certain travel expenses in a manner that is most effective and efficient for the agency. As stated in *Part IV: Before You Travel* under Agency Responsibilities, agencies are required to have written established policies based on the various statutes outlined in 5 U.S.C. Chapter 57, on which form the conditions for payment of travel allowances in the FTR are based. Having clear written policies makes it easier to determine a traveler's entitlement when compared with any stated condition on a travel authorization. For example, IRS travel policy states in part that a GPS may be reimbursed "if the GPS is permanently affixed to the vehicle and the charge for the GPS is included in the daily rate rental car fee. Portable GPS devices are not considered to be standard equipment, but an accessory so you would be liable for any costs if the device is lost or stolen."

In the case of CBCA 1899-TRAV, *In the Matter of Terris King* (July 26, 2010), on eight occasions while on travel, the claimant paid a surcharge to rent a navigation system in a vehicle. Because the claimant lacked express authorization to expend additional funds for the rental of a navigation system, the claimant was determined to be personally liable for the associated amounts.

156 Can a traveler be reimbursed car rental damage fees if the car was not rented through the government?

The traveler may be liable for car rental damages and should consult with his/her agency's legal counsel. Travelers should rent cars through the U.S. Government Rental Car and Truck Program managed by the Defense Travel Management Office (DTMO). Under certain conditions, travelers may obtain rates directly through the rental car company website, toll-free numbers, or walk-up services, but in those cases the traveler is responsible for and must ensure that he/she is booking a government rate or that the government administrative rate supplement (GARS) is included.

157 What is the government administrative rate supplement?

The government administrative rate supplement (GARS) is a $5.00 mandatory fee charged to the renter per day worldwide. GARS is intended to address those costs incurred by the rental car company that are particular to doing business with the government (such as under-aged drivers, additional drivers, and administration).

158 Is a traveler required to rent a vehicle through the DTMO rental program?

As stated on the DTMO website, the program provides "special rental benefits and reduced rates to all federal government employees traveling on official business. The programs are designed to meet the needs of the federal traveler, and provide quality rentals through a variety of companies at over 10,000 rental locations." Further information about the U.S. Rental Car and Truck Program is provided on the DTMO website: www.defensetravel.dod.mil/Docs/CarRentalAgreement.pdf.

If a rental car is not available through the government rental program, the traveler should consider using a government vehicle. Otherwise, the traveler may be liable for any or all damages to a rental car not rented through the DTMO.

In CBCA 1207-TRAV, *In the Matter of Marian Roche* (Sept. 23, 2008), an employee of the National Security Agency (NSA) rented a car to travel to a conference in Texas. Rather than use the agency's contract travel office (CTO), Omega World Travel, she rented the car from E-Z Rent-A-Car.

When Roche returned the car, the rental company discovered a scratch on the left front door and charged her $1039.69 for the damage. NSA refused to reimburse her for the fee on the basis that she had used an unauthorized CTO. It limited her entitlement to Omega World Travel's daily rate.

Roche took her claim to the CBCA, maintaining that NSA's travel office had advised her that she could make her own car reservation. She also asserted that "when making travel arrangements thru the CTO, I [was] asked (as are all other travelers) whether we want the CTO to make car and/or hotel reservations." Roche believed that the question implied that use of the CTO is optional.

The CBCA found that NSA was correct to limit her reimbursement to the cost of renting a car from the CTO. JTR section

2102-B.1.a states unequivocally that "it is mandatory to obtain a rental vehicle through the CTO . . . when available."

Furthermore, the rate charged by rental car companies contracting with the government includes full liability and vehicle loss and damage for the traveler and the government. In situations where the CTO is not used, JTR section C2102-B.3 provides that "reimbursement is limited to what it would have cost if a CTO . . . had made the rental vehicle arrangements."

For civilian federal workers, the rules are the same under the FTR. Section 301-50.8 provides that "when authorized to use a rental vehicle under Sec. 301-10.450 of this chapter, you must rent a vehicle from a vendor that participates in the Surface Deployment and Distribution Command (SDDC) U.S. government Car Rental Agreement, unless you are OCONUS and no agreement is in place for your TDY location. SDDC has negotiated rental car agreements that include automatic unlimited mileage, collision damage insurance, and ceiling rates."

Furthermore, FTR section 301-10.453 specifies that federal employees "are responsible for any additional cost resulting from the unauthorized use of a commercial rental automobile for other than official travel-related purposes."

159 If a traveler is involved in a car accident before or after work hours with an authorized rental car and did not take out collision insurance (in accordance with agency policy), who is liable for the cost of the repairs?

If authorized, employees may use a rental car not only to and from lodging to TDY, but also to places of worship and for dining. However, if food is available at the traveler's lodging facility, the agency may determine that the rental car was being used for other than official business and therefore was not authorized (unless the traveler required a special meal for religious or medical reasons). In that case, the traveler would be responsible and would not be reimbursed for damage to the rental car while it was being used before or after work hours for other than official business.

Having clear written agency policy would avoid such financial liability to the traveler. The traveler may seek to obtain advance authorization to use a rental car for dining, for example, as a condition for travel on the travel authorization.

160 If a traveler is authorized to extend TDY for personal reasons and retains the rental car, is the government or the traveler liable for damages to the car in the case of an accident?

Similarly, the traveler may not be reimbursed for the cost of repairs since the traveler was not on official duty at the time of the accident.

In GSBCA 16477-TRAV, *In the Matter of Tassos Abadiotakis* (October 13, 2004), an employee of NASA in Cape Canaveral, Florida, was authorized TDY in Ogden, Utah. NASA approved commercial airfare and the use of a rental car for the assignment.

Abadiotakis' trip was scheduled to begin on Wednesday, June 9, and end on Friday, June 11. Shortly before departing, Abadiotakis advised NASA that he wanted to travel to Jackson Hole, Wyoming, following the conclusion of his assignment for personal business. As a result, the agency revised his return date to Sunday, June 13.

Abadiotakis drove the rental car to Jackson for the weekend after completing his TDY. While returning to Ogden at 4:00 a.m. for his return flight home at 10:00 a.m., he hit an elk. Abadiotakis was not injured, but the car was damaged.

The rental car company billed Abadiotakis $2,627.77 for repairing the vehicle. Apparently, this amount represented the collision deductible.

Abadiotakis asked NASA to reimburse him that cost. Uncertain whether it could pay the expense, the agency requested an advance decision from the GSBCA.

The board found that the agency could not reimburse him. It emphasized that FTR section 301-2.2 provides that an agency may pay only those expenses that are essential to the transaction of official business. In addition, it noted that FTR section 301-10.451 provides that employees may be paid only "deductible amounts paid by [an employee]. . . if the damage occurred while [the employee was] performing official business."

In this case, the accident did not occur while Abadiotakis was performing official business. In fact, the GSBCA explained that if Abadiotakis had returned as originally scheduled, the incident would not have taken place. Therefore, any expenses Abadiotakis incurred in using the rental car after Friday were his responsibility.

In a similar case, GAO was confronted with the same issue with comparable facts. However, in that case, GAO authorized reimbursement. Why the different result? The employee's use of the car occurred while "on official government business."

In the case of *Raymond B. Washburn*, B-231082, 68 Comp. Gen. 318 (1989), an employee of the Army Missile Command at Redstone Arsenal, Huntsville, Alabama, was authorized travel to a conference in Orlando, Florida. His orders approved the use of a commercial rental car.

Washburn rented an automobile from Budget Rent-A-Car upon arriving in Orlando. He did not obtain any extra insurance to provide full collision coverage.

The conference ended on April 10. Washburn, however, was not scheduled to return to his permanent duty station until the next day. As a result, he joined other conference attendees for dinner that night, leaving his rental car parked at the Marriott hotel where the meetings had been held. After dinner he was dropped off at his place of lodging, the Hilton Inn. He then remembered that his rental car was still parked at the Marriott, three blocks from the Hilton. Since he and other government employees who had attended the meetings were leaving the Hilton for the airport the following morning in the rental car, he decided to walk to the Marriott and drive the car back to the Hilton parking lot.

While driving from the Marriott parking lot in the rain at 2:00 a.m., Washburn attempted to turn on the windshield wipers and, while looking at the instrument panel, struck the rear of a parked van, substantially damaging the front passenger side of the rental car.

The rental car company billed Washburn $2,100. GAO found that the Army could pay the expense because the accident occurred while

Washburn was performing official government business. It explained that the collision occurred while Washburn was driving the rental car from the meeting place to his hotel after having his evening meal. According to GAO, it was essential to the transaction of official business that "the rental vehicle be returned to Washburn's place of lodging so that he and the other government employees staying at the Hilton would be able to depart for the airport later on the morning of April 11."

161 Does the government have a policy on texting while operating an authorized vehicle while on official travel?

Yes. Executive Order 13513, Federal Leadership on Reducing Text Messaging While Driving, was issued on October 1, 2009. Section 2 states in part that "federal employees shall not engage in text messaging (a) when driving GOV, or when driving POV while on official government business, or (b) when using electronic equipment supplied by the government while driving."

In part, Section 3 directs agencies "(i) to take appropriate measures to implement this order, (ii) to adopt measures to ensure compliance with section 2 of this order, including through appropriate disciplinary actions, and (iii) to notify the Secretary of Transportation of the measures it undertakes hereunder."

162 Can a traveler be reimbursed the fee to unlock an authorized rental car while on official travel?

No, locked-car fees are not reimbursable.

In the CBCA case *In the Matter of Lindsay Hum,* CBCA 2277-TRAV (Mar. 29, 2011), a Navy civilian employee locked herself out of her rental car while on official travel. She appealed to the CBCA seeking reimbursement for the $55 charge billed by the rental car agency to get back into the car. The CBCA denied her claim.

FTR section 01-2.2 authorizes agencies to pay only those expenses considered essential to conducting official business. The CBCA has previously found that costs associated with entry into a locked vehicle are not essential travel expenses and that locksmith services necessitated by a traveler's own error are not reimbursable.

In another case, *Billy M. Battles*, CBCA 1568-TRAV (July 16, 2009), a Food and Drug Administration employee locked himself out of an agency-issued car while performing official duties. Unable to unlock the automobile himself, he called a locksmith to open it, at a cost of $50. Battles submitted a claim to his agency for reimbursement of the locksmith fee, noting that he needed to unlock the car to retrieve equipment that was necessary to perform an investigation. His claim was denied.

In its decision regarding Battles' claim, the CBCA noted that in reimbursing official local travel expenses, agencies may pay only expenses that are considered "essential to the transaction of official business." (FTR 301-2.2) In this case, the locksmith fee was not incurred in the performance of official business, but instead by Battles' own mistake in locking himself out of the car. Moreover, the cost of a locksmith does not qualify as a reimbursable miscellaneous expense under FTR section 301-12.1.

The CBCA's reasoning was based largely on a previous decision issued by GAO regarding a similar issue. In *Robert Berman*, B-210928 (Apr. 22, 1983), a NASA employee locked his keys in a rental car while on official travel and protested the denial of his claim for locksmith services. In determining that Berman was not eligible for reimbursement, GAO explained: "Mr. Berman's action in locking himself out of his car was the proximate cause of his incurring the locksmith fee and, hence, the fee cannot be regarded as essential to the transacting of official business."

MEALS

Travelers are entitled to expenses incurred for breakfast, lunch, dinner, and related tips and taxes. Travelers are not entitled to reimbursement for alcoholic beverage and entertainment expenses, nor for any expenses incurred for other persons. Travelers are required to exclude those expenses from their vouchers.

163 When should per diem be adjusted for meals?

Per diem should be adjusted when a meal is paid for by the government, for example, when a meal is provided as a part of a conference or registration fee. Per diem is not adjusted for complimentary meals provided on a common carrier or at a hotel if there is no additional charge for the meal in the lodging cost.

For example, say a traveler attends a conference that includes three meals as a part of the conference fee. The traveler chooses not to consume two of the meals and purchases meals separate from the conference. Not only will the traveler's M&IE per diem be reduced to reflect the conference-provided meals, but reimbursement for the separately purchased meals will be denied.

In accordance with FTR section 301-11.18(a), a federal employee is required to deduct any government-furnished meal included in a registration or conference fee. At your agency's discretion, you may claim full M&IE allowance if you meet the criteria stated in FTR section 301-11.18(b) or (c), which address meal deductions for medical, religious, or official business reasons. However, specific authorization or prior approval is required in accordance with FTR section 301-2.5(p).

Regarding complimentary meals provided by a common carrier or hotel, in CBCA 1900-TRAV, *In the Matter of W. Lynn Hodges* (May 3, 2010), the Department of Agriculture deducted the value of four breakfast meals from the travel claim of an employee who had traveled to Philadelphia on TDY. The breakfast meals had been provided as complimentary by the hotel where Hodges stayed. The hotel offered a complimentary breakfast to every federal employee staying at the hotel; this offer was advertised on various websites.

The agency cited FTR section 301-11.18 as the basis for deducting the meals, arguing that the meals were provided by the government in connection with an agency meeting.

In reviewing the case, the CBCA found no evidence that the agency specifically negotiated or paid for the breakfasts in question. The letter of intent between the agency and the hotel for the agency meeting listed breakfast as being furnished to the agency's employees on a complimentary basis. The CBCA therefore found that the breakfasts were indeed complimentary.

FTR section 301-11.17 provides: "A meal provided by a common carrier or a complimentary meal provided by a hotel/motel does not affect your per diem." Because the breakfasts had been provided at no cost to the agency, the CBCA found that the agency could not deduct them from the employee's claim. The CBCA directed the Department of Agriculture to repay the deduction to Hodges.

164 What are the exceptions for not deducting a furnished meal?

Your agency, at its discretion, may allow you to claim the full M&IE allowance if:

- You were unable to consume the furnished meals because of medical requirements or religious beliefs
- In accordance with administrative procedures prescribed by your agency, you requested specific approval to claim the full M&IE allowance prior to your travel
- In accordance with administrative procedures prescribed by your agency, you made a reasonable effort to make alternative meal arrangements but were unable to do so
- You purchased substitute meals in accordance with your medical requirements or religious beliefs
- You were unable to take part in a government-furnished meal due to the conduct of official business.

165 Can an agency pay the costs of meals and light refreshments during training or a meeting at the permanent duty station?

As a general rule, without specific statutory authority, employees may not be paid subsistence expense or furnished free meals by the government at their permanent duty station. However, an exception to this prohibition is provided under 5 U.S.C. 4110 (1988), which states: "Appropriations available to an agency for travel expenses are available for expenses of attendance at meetings which are concerned with the functions or activities for which the appropriation is made or which will contribute to improved conduct, supervision, or management of the functions or activities."

Therefore, an agency may pay for food at conferences and events when the cost is included as an incidental and is nonseparable from the registration or attendance fee under the Government Employees Training Act (5 U.S.C. 4109 and 4110), regardless of the employee's location. If the cost of the food is separable or is not included in the registration or attendance fee, the agency head may determine that the meal is a necessary expense in order to obtain the full benefit of the event.

Those in a travel status will have their per diem reduced as stated in question #163 in accordance with FTR section 301-11.18, and those not in a travel status will be entitled to have the meals and snacks as an integral part of the meeting.

MISCELLANEOUS & INCIDENTAL EXPENSES

Miscellaneous and incidental expenses are intended to cover certain necessary travel and transportation-related expenses incurred for official business.

The following items may be reimbursed as a miscellaneous expense when they have been authorized or approved by your agency. In addition, lodging taxes are reimbursable when lodging is authorized and is not related to foreign travel.

General expenses	Fees to obtain money	Special expenses of foreign travel
Baggage expenses as described in FTR 301-12.2 Services of guides, interpreters, drivers Services of an attendant as described in §301-13.3 Use of computers, printers, faxing machines, and scanners Services of typists, data processors, or stenographers Storage of property used on official business Hire of conference center room or hotel room for official business Official telephone calls/service. Faxes, telegrams, cablegrams, or radiograms Lodging taxes as prescribed in §301-11.27 Laundry, cleaning and pressing of clothing expenses as prescribed in §301-11.31 Energy surcharge and lodging resort fee(s) (when such fee(s) is/are not optional)	Fees for traveler's checks Fees for money orders Fees for certified checks Transaction fees for use of automated teller machines (ATMs)—government contractor-issued charge card	Commissions on conversion of foreign currency Passport and/or visa fees, including fees for a physical examination if one is required to obtain a passport and/or visa and such examination could not be obtained at a government facility. Reimbursement for such fees may include travel and transportation costs to the passport/visa issuing office if located outside the local commuting area of the employee's official station and the traveler's presence at that office is mandatory. Costs of photographs for passports and visas Foreign country exit fees Costs of birth, health, and identity certificates Charges for inoculations that cannot be obtained through a federal dispensary

166 What baggage fees are reimbursable?

Agencies may reimburse the following baggage expenses:

- Transportation charges for authorized excess.
- Necessary charges for transferring baggage.
- Necessary charges for storage of baggage when such charges are the result of official business.
- All fees pertaining to the first checked bag. In addition, charges relating to the second and subsequent bags may be reimbursed when the agency determines that those expenses are necessary and in the interest of the government.
- Charges or tips at transportation terminals for handling government property carried by the traveler.

Agencies must establish policies and procedures regarding who determines when excess baggage is necessary for official travel.

167 Is curbside baggage check-in a reimbursable expense?

No. Curbside baggage check-in is considered a personal convenience, and the traveler is therefore responsible for the fee.

168 If a traveler's luggage does not arrive at the TDY destination, can the traveler be authorized to purchase toiletries and necessary clothing in order to attend a meeting representing his/her agency?

Unless your agency has specific provisions under its appropriations act or other legislation, it may not use appropriated funds to purchase toiletries and articles of personal clothing that may be retained for personal use. The GSBCA, however, has ruled that clothing does not qualify as a "necessary" or "miscellaneous" expense.

In GSBCA 15030-TRAV, *In the Matter of Thomas J. May* (July 29, 1999), a civilian employee of the Air Force flew to Tyndall Air

Force Base on a military aircraft to complete a TDY assignment. He arrived on a Sunday. Unfortunately, the Air Force misplaced May's suitcase. As a result, he had no spare clothing for his first day of work on Monday.

May started his TDY assignment wearing the same clothes he had arrived in the day before. That evening he purchased a pair of pants and three shirts. The Air Force subsequently located May's luggage and returned it to him on Tuesday.

After returning from his TDY, May submitted a voucher for the cost of the clothing he had purchased. He argued that the clothes should qualify as a miscellaneous expense under paragraph C4709 of the JTR. The Air Force refused to reimburse the expense, so May appealed to the GSBCA.

The GSBCA agreed with the Air Force's rejection of the voucher. According to the JTR, military services may reimburse employees only for miscellaneous expenses that are "incurred during the performance of their temporary duties in connection with the transaction of official business."

The JTR identifies several miscellaneous expenses for which employees may be reimbursed: (1) use of computers and printers, (2) hiring a typist or stenographer, (3) renting storage, and (4) traveler check and passport fees. The GSBCA emphasized that each of these expenses provides a direct and primary benefit to the government. May's purchase of clothing, however, did not primarily benefit the government; rather, May could use the clothing for his own personal benefit. To support its ruling, the board cited decisions from the Comptroller General (CG), which held jurisdiction over travel appeals before the GSBCA assumed that role in 1996. In several cases, the CG had ruled that employees could not be reimbursed for renting clothing while on travel. According to the CG, employees should not be reimbursed for items while on travel that they would normally have to purchase to perform their duties at their permanent location.

The GSBCA found no reason to treat the purchase of new clothing differently from the precedent set by the CG for renting the same items.

169 Is there a minimum or maximum for reimbursement of tips? Can an agency reimburse less than what the traveler actually spent on tips?

In accordance with FTR section 301-10.421, an agency has discretion to determine a reasonable amount for tips. Therefore, an employee may not be reimbursed the full amount spent on tips if that amount exceeds the amount the agency considers "reasonable."

170 When can an agency disallow payment of a claimed item?

An agency can disallow payment of a claimed item if a traveler does not provide proper itemization of an expense; does not provide a receipt or other documentation required to support the traveler's claim; or claims an expense that is not authorized.

171 What will the agency do when it disallows an expense?

The agency will issue the employee a notice of disallowance and will pay the claim for those items that are allowed.

172 What must a traveler do to challenge a disallowed expense?

The traveler must:

- File a new claim
- Provide full itemization for all disallowed items reclaimed
- Provide receipts for all disallowed items reclaimed that require receipts (unless the agency already has the receipt)
- Provide a copy of the notice of disallowance
- State the proper authority for the claim if you are challenging the agency's application of the law or statute
- Follow your agency's procedures for challenging disallowed claims.

If after reconsideration by your agency your claim is still denied, you may submit your claim for adjudication to the GSA Board of Contract Appeals in accordance with 48 CFR part 6104.

WHEN TRAVEL IS INTERRUPTED

Unfortunately, official travel is sometimes interrupted for an emergency. Interrupted travel is usually defined as "emergency" travel that results from:

- Your becoming incapacitated by illness or injury not due to your own misconduct
- The death or serious illness of a member of your family
- A catastrophic occurrence or impending disaster, such as fire, flood, or act of God that directly affects your home.

> If you have to interrupt or discontinue your TDY travel, contact your travel authorizing/approving official for instructions as soon as possible.

173 Who is considered to be "family" with respect to emergency travel?

"Family" includes any member of your immediate family as defined in FTR section 300-3.1. However, your agency may, on a case-by-case basis, expand this definition to include other members of your or your spouse's or domestic partner's extended family.

174 When an illness or injury occurs on TDY, what expenses are allowed?

Your agency may pay:

- Per diem at the location where you were treated for incapacitating illness or injury for a reasonable period of time (generally

14 calendar days). However, your agency may choose to pay for a longer period.

- Transportation and per diem expense for travel to an alternate location to receive medical treatment.
- Transportation and per diem expenses to return to your official station.
- Transportation costs of a medically necessary attendant.

FTR section 301-70.501 allows the continuance of per diem "when an employee interrupts a travel assignment because of an incapacitating illness or injury." FTR section 301-70.502 prohibits reimbursement if "confinement in a hospital or medical facility that is within the proximity of the official station or is the same one the employee would have been admitted to if the illness or injury had occurred while at the official station and/or the government provides or reimburses the employee for hospitalization under any federal statute (including hospitalization in a Department of Veterans Affairs (VA) medical center or military hospital) other than 5 U.S.C. 8901-8913 (Federal Employees Health Benefits program)."

PART VI

When You Return from Travel

Upon return from official travel, you are required to submit a travel claim or voucher—an itemized statement of expenses incurred while on official travel.

175 When is a traveler required to submit a travel claim?

Under FTR section 301-52.7, travelers must submit a travel claim (voucher) within five working days after completion of the trip or period of travel or every 30 days if the employee is on continuous travel status. There is no exception to this rule; an agency may require submission within fewer days but not more.

176 What must a traveler provide with a travel claim?

A traveler must provide evidence of travel authorizations, including any necessary special authorizations, receipts for lodging regardless of the amount, and receipts for any other expense over $75.

177 What can a traveler do if a receipt is lost or misplaced?

The failure to furnish receipts as required must be fully explained on the travel voucher. Mere inconvenience in the matter of collecting receipts is not acceptable. In some cases, such as for a lodging receipt, the traveler may be able to obtain a duplicate receipt.

178 When are receipts required?

You must provide a lodging receipt regardless of the amount paid. You must also provide a receipt for any authorized expense over $75 or provide a reason acceptable to your agency explaining why you are unable to furnish the necessary receipts. Your agency may exempt an expenditure from the receipt requirement because the expenditure is confidential. However, your agency may require receipts for any amount.

179 How long should receipts be retained?

Receipts must be retained for six years and three months as prescribed by the National Archives and Records Administration (NARA) (see http://www.archives.gov/records-mgmt/grs/grs09.html or NARA Transmittal No. 22 dated April 2010).

180 If a traveler does not submit a receipt for an expense or lists an unauthorized expense on the voucher, can the agency disallow the expense? Can a traveler appeal the disallowance?

FTR section 301-52.8 provides the authority for an approving official to disallow an expense. The agency is required to provide the traveler a notice of the disallowance in writing (FTR section 301-52.9). A traveler may then request that the agency reconsider the disallowance (FTR section 301-52.10). If the claim is denied after reconsideration, the traveler may further challenge the disallowance to the CBCA (FTR section 301-52.11(g)).

181 A traveler's travel voucher is often submitted by an agency-authorized alternate preparer. Is it legal for this individual to sign a traveler's voucher?

The traveler's electronic signature on the travel voucher certifies the accuracy of all items being claimed and also that each claim was used in conducting official business. The validity of a signed voucher or any part thereof is the responsibility of the traveler.

Although an alternate preparer may prepare, sign, and submit a travel claim on a traveler's behalf, the traveler is still required to "certify that the claim is true and correct to the best of his/her knowledge and belief, and that payment or credit has not been received by him/her." Any falsification of an item in your claim may be considered action to defraud the government. Should this occur, you forfeit reimbursement pursuant to 28 U.S.C. 2514 and you may be subject under 18 U.S.C. 287 and 1010 to a fine of not more than $10,000 or imprisonment for not more than five years or both.

182 How are "constructive costs" calculated?

The FTR and the JTR permit employees to travel by a means other than the mode the government determines is in its best interest. However, if an employee chooses to travel by an alternate means, an agency is not required to reimburse all of the employee's actual expenses. Rather, an agency may pay the employee's travel expenses up to the "constructive total" the agency would have incurred had the employee used the transportation mode most advantageous to the government.

For example, in GSBCA 15109-TRAV, *In the Matter of Russell E. Yates* (November 30, 1999), a computer engineer for NASA in Houston, Texas, was temporarily assigned to perform software testing in Tampa, Florida, from March 15 to March 19. The agency determined that traveling by air was the "most advantageous form of transportation to the government." Despite this finding, Yates chose to drive to Tampa in his motorhome.

He departed Houston on March 13, arrived in Tampa on March 14, completed his TDY, and returned to Houston on March 19. While in Tampa, Yates stayed in his motorhome at a mobile home campground.

NASA reimbursed Yates his transportation costs up to the cost of roundtrip airfare between Houston and Tampa. In addition, the agency reimbursed his meal and incidental expenses according to the applicable per diem rate for Tampa. The agency, however, reimbursed him the actual cost of the mobile home campground fees rather than the constructive cost of a hotel room. Yates appealed to the GSBCA, arguing that he was entitled to estimated hotel costs.

The board agreed and, as part of its published opinion, established a formula for calculating constructive costs. The GSBCA explained that when an employee chooses to travel by a mode other than the means of transportation most advantageous to the government, agencies must calculate the employee's travel costs in two separate ways. First, the agency should determine the allowability of the various components of an employee's travel claim using the standard application of FTR section 301-70.105(a). The agency should then total the allowable costs. Second, the agency should determine the total constructive cost of the employee's travel had he/she traveled by the method of transportation deemed to be in the government's best interest.

After computing the totals, the agency should compare them. If the total of costs determined in the standard fashion to be allowable is greater than the total of the constructive costs, the agency should limit reimbursement to the latter figure.

183 If a traveler has a contractor-issued government travel charge card, what is the required method for reimbursement?

Travelers who are issued an individually billed account (IBA) for a contractor-issued government travel charge card must use split pay (disbursement) to pay all government travel charge card expenses when submitting a voucher for reimbursement of travel and travel-related expenses. Cardholders are responsible for paying all charges and fees associated with the IBA travel charge card in full by the billing due date whether or not the cardholder has been reimbursed by the agency.

184 What is "split pay" or "split disbursement" and how can an exemption be obtained?

Split disbursement is the process of dividing a travel voucher reimbursement between the charge card vendor and the traveler. The balance owed to each is sent directly to the applicable party.

Section 4.4 in Appendix B of OMB Circular A-123 states in part that "where individual cardholders are responsible for making payments to the charge card vendor, charge card managers are required to implement split disbursement and salary offset procedures for travel charge card programs." Under Section 4.4.3 in Appendix B, "agencies may request exemptions when they determine that the cost of implementing split disbursement and/or salary offset exceeds the benefits. Agency heads must request such exemptions from the Director of the Office of Management and Budget (OMB) in writing, and provide the reasons therein."

185 What authority requires the use of split disbursement, which is not required by the FTR?

Although it appears that FTR section 301-70.708(h) does not require the use of split disbursement, agencies are required to comply with OMB Circular A-123, Appendix B. Appendix B, which applies to all executive branch departments and agencies, mandates split disbursement for travel charge cardholders unless an agency has an approved waiver or exemption.

186 What happens if a traveler is late paying the charges on his/her IBA?

Cardholders are required to make payment for all undisputed charges on their travel charge card bill in full by the statement billing due date (25 to 30 days after the closing date on the billing statement). The due date is printed on the bill. Failure to pay the monthly bill in a timely manner may result in the loss of charging privileges. If the cardholder's card is suspended, he/she will be unable to use it until the bank receives payment. If the cardholder's card is canceled due to non-payment, the delinquency may be reported to credit bureaus, referred to collection agencies, or lead to other collection actions. The cardholder may not be eligible to receive a new card account.

Upon written request from the bank, the agency may collect, from the employee's disposable pay, any undisputed delinquent amount that is owed to the issuing bank.

187 What is disposable pay?

Disposable pay is is the part of the employee's compensation remaining after the deduction of any amounts required by law to be withheld. These deductions do not include discretionary deductions such as savings bonds, charitable contributions, etc. Deductions may be made from any type of pay (e.g., basic pay, special pay, retirement pay, incentive pay).

These deductions do not include discretionary deductions such as savings bonds, charitable contributions, etc. Deductions may be made from any type of pay you receive from your agency, including basic pay, special pay, retirement pay, or incentive pay.

188 What is the maximum amount an agency may collect from an employee's disposable pay?

As set forth in Public Law 105-264, 112 Stat. 2350 (October 19, 1998), the maximum amount your agency may deduct from your disposable pay is 15 percent each pay period, unless you agree in writing to a larger percentage.

189 What can an IBA cardholder do if he/she notices an erroneous charge?

Under the SmartPay2 Master Contract, as an IBA cardholder, you are responsible for payment of the activity on your travel charge card. If you notice an erroneous charge, contact your bank immediately to dispute the charge and follow the procedures outlined in your agreement. Your bank will issue you a temporary credit for the disputed amount until a determination is made whether or not it is a valid charge.

If you do not follow the procedures outlined in your agreement, the charge may be considered "undisputed." If you do not pay the undisputed amount, your travel charge card may be suspended or canceled. The bank may also initiate collection action for the undisputed charge. If your travel charge card is canceled due to non-payment, the delinquency may be reported to credit bureaus as stated in question #186. The bank is under no obligation to reissue you another travel charge card.

190 Is an agency required to reimburse a traveler who refuses reimbursement?

Yes. Per diem is authorized under 5 U.S.C. 5702, and FTR section 301-11.3 requires that either the daily allowance (per diem) or actual and necessary expenses be paid for expenses incurred while traveling on official business. However, an employee is not required to accept reimbursement according to GSBCA 15057-TRAV, which states in part: "we know of no way to force an employee to accept reimbursement for travel costs." It should also be noted that although a traveler has six years and three months to file a claim, the traveler is required to file a claim in accordance with FTR section 301-52.7 and agency policy. Failure to do so may result in disciplinary action for failure to follow agency policy, which is based on the FTR and 5 U.S.C. Chapter 57.

PART VII

Conferences

When planning a conference, a government employee must:

- Minimize all conference costs, including administrative costs, conference attendees' travel costs, and conference attendees' time costs
- Maximize the use of government-owned or government-provided conference facilities to the extent possible
- Identify opportunities to reduce costs in selecting a particular conference location and facility (e.g., through the availability of lower rates during the off-season at a site with seasonal rates)
- Ensure that the conference planner or designee does not retain for personal use any promotional benefits or materials received from a travel service provider as a result of booking the conference
- Develop and establish internal policies to ensure these standards are met.

In addition to complying with FTR section 301-74, under Executive Order 13589, each agency, agency component, and office of inspector general is required to "designate a senior-level official to be responsible for developing and implementing policies and controls to ensure efficient spending on travel and conference-related activities." OMB has further directed agencies to take practical steps to improve operations, increase efficiency, and cut unnecessary spending.

191 What are the definitions of a conference, meeting, and training?

A *conference* is defined as a symposium, seminar, workshop, or other organized or formal meeting, lasting portions of one or more days, whether conducted face-to-face or through the use of information technology, where individuals assemble to exchange information and views or explore or clarify a defined subject, problem, or area of knowledge, whether or not a published report results from such meeting. The term may include training activities that meet the definition of training under the government Employees Training Act, 5 U.S.C. 4101(4). The term does not include technical and administrative site visits, whether conducted face-to-face or through the use of information technology. (Appendix C to the FTR (Amendment 2009-05 dated August 20, 2009.) A *meeting* is an assembly of persons to discuss general matters as part of a course of doing business, which is held in federal or non-federal space.

Training is defined as the process of providing for and making available to an employee, and placing or enrolling the employee in a planned, prepared, and coordinated program, course, curriculum, subject, system, or routine of instruction or education, in scientific, professional, technical, mechanical, trade, clerical, fiscal, administrative, or other fields, which will improve individual and organizational performance and assist in achieving the agency's mission and performance goals (5 U.S.C. Chapter 41-Training, 4101).

192 What cost-saving tools are available to government conference planners?

Two free government tools are available to government conference planners:

The GSA travel management information service (MIS) tool is an easy way for agencies to manage travel dollars and procure travel at lower prices, while also helping manage travel policy compliance. Agencies may also use the Travel MIS tool to find the most environmentally and economically practical accommodations for conferences or meetings using per diem rates and City Pair fares.

This tool is available at the GSA website www.gsa.gov/travelmis.

In addition, GSA's website www.fedrooms.com has a Groups and Meetings tool to help identify a single hotel that meets all the needs of the conference and does so quickly, anonymously, and within policy.

193 Can an agency provide a conference "memory" book to conference attendees?

GAO has long held that appropriated funds may be used for objects not specifically set forth in an appropriation action only if there is a direct connection between such objects and the purpose for which the appropriation was made. In addition, the object must be reasonably related to the carrying out of such purpose. Memory books do not meet these criteria.

194 Can an agency hosting a conference provide meals to non-federal employees?

No; the Government Employees Training Act does not apply to non-federal personnel. Appropriations are not available to pay for food unless specifically authorized or the agency can demonstrate that such expenditures are an essential, constituent part of accomplishing an authorized agency function.

195 Can an employee be reimbursed the cost of renting or purchasing formal attire that will be worn as a part of the employee's performance of official duties?

No. According to GAO decision B-215222 (October 11, 1984), the cost of formal attire is not a reimbursable expense even for events attended as part of an employee's official duties.

196 What is the definition of light refreshments?

GSA defines light refreshments as "modest items of food and drink that are offered other than as a part of a meal." FTR section

301-74.11 provides a list that includes coffee, tea, milk, juice, soft drinks, donuts, bagels, fruit, pretzels, cookies, and muffins.

197 May a federal conference planner keep for personal use any promotional benefits or materials he/she receives from a travel service provider?

No. Promotional benefits or materials a federal conference planner receives from a travel service provider in connection with planning or scheduling an official conference or other group travel (as opposed to personally performing official travel) are considered the property of the government. The conference planner may accept the benefits or materials only on behalf of the federal government

198 Why is budgeting important to conference planning?

The goal of budgeting in conferenece planning is to minimize total costs, including sustainability and environmental impacts as well as dollars. Conference planners should work with their agency's chief financial officer to ensure proper fund management and involve the contracting officer and contracting officer's technical representative to ensure that all written agreements and decisions are in accordance with applicable rules and regulations. Involving these agency representatives may help eliminate excessive spending on conferences.

Additional information on lessons learned concerning the importance of conference planning and involving the appropriate agency officials is provided in two recent inspector general audits of conferences: *Management Deficiency Report*, General Services Administration, Public Buildings Service, 2010 Western Regions Conference (April 2, 2012); and *Audit of Department of Justice Conference Planning and Food and Beverage Costs*, U.S. Department of Justice, Office of the Inspector General, Audit Division, Audit Report 11-43 (revised version issued October 2011).

199 How can an agency mitigate the risk of inappropriate spending practices for conferences?

OMB Memorandum M-11-35, Eliminating Excess Conference Spending and Promoting Efficiency in Government, requires each agency to have a senior-level official (deputy secretary or equivalent) approve conference-related activities and expenses until the agency certifies that policies and controls are in place to mitigate the risk of inappropriate spending practices with regard to conferences.

OMB Memorandum M-12-12 expands on the requirements of OMB Memorandum M-11-35 by requiring agencies to:

- Ensure that conference expenses and activities comply with the FTR directives and executive branch policies on conferences as well as the Federal Acquisition Regulation (FAR) requirements on contracting goods and services
- Have senior-level review of all planned conferences
- Have senior-level approval of all future conference expenses in excess of $100,000
- Prohibit expenses in excess of $500,000 on a single conference
- Report publicly on all conference expenses in excess of $100,000.

By January 31 of each year beginning in 2013, agencies are required to provide the following information for each conference held:

- Total expenses incurred by the agency for the conference
- Location of the conference
- Date of the conference
- Brief explanation of how the conference advanced the mission of the agency
- Total number of individuals whose travel expenses or other conference expenses were paid by the agency.

For further information about the requirements, including reporting requirements, contact your agency's travel manager.

PART VIII

Memberships in Travel Rewards Programs

Public Law 107-107 allows government travelers to retain a promotional item for personal or business use if the promotional item is obtained under the same terms as those offered to the general public and at no additional cost to the federal government. For example, an employee may keep a prize won in a contest or lottery sponsored by an air carrier if the contest was open to the general public and was not limited to ticket-holding passengers.

However, if you are offered promotional or travel benefits as a result of your role as a conference or group travel planner or if you were involuntarily prevented from boarding an aircraft while holding a valid transportation ticket, you may not retain those benefits for your personal use. You may accept such benefits only on behalf of the federal government and those benefits may only be used for official government business.

200 Who owns the compensation provided by an airline if a traveler either voluntarily gives up his/her seat or is involuntarily prevented from boarding the aircraft ("bumped")?

The reimbursement an employee may receive depends on whether he/she was forced to give up the seat or did so voluntarily.

In GSBCA 15523-TRAV, *In the Matter of Brian E. Havitz (August 15, 2001)*, a civilian employee of the National Guard Service of the Army and Air Force in Blue Ash, Ohio, was authorized for a TDY assignment in Utah. Havitz's agency purchased round-trip airfare for the assignment. His flight itinerary included a layover in Chicago on his return flight. After completing his assignment, Havitz departed Salt Lake City and landed in Chicago. Unfortunately, he was unable to take the connecting flight to Ohio because it had been overbooked. Instead of taking a later flight that day or staying over in Chicago and catching a flight the next day, Havitz rented a car and drove home.

Havitz turned in the unused portion of his ticket when he returned to work. In addition, he submitted a voucher for reimbursement of the rental car. Uncertain whether it could approve his request, his agency requested an opinion from the GSBCA.

The GSBCA stated that it needed more information to reach a decision. Specifically, the board needed to know whether Havitz voluntarily relinquished his seat on the overbooked flight or if he was denied boarding.

FTR section 301-10.117 permits employees to voluntarily vacate a seat on a flight if doing so will not interfere with official duties. The employee, however, must bear any additional expenses.

When an employee is "bumped" involuntarily, the employee is generally entitled to reimbursement for additional subsistence costs that may be incurred, but is required to ensure that any remuneration provided by the airline is made payable to the "Treasurer of the United States." (FTR 301-10.116) The GSBCA noted that GAO has previously ruled that the rationale underlying this provision is that the government has contracted with the airline for the service and therefore is entitled to compensation for the non-performance of the service as a form of liquidated damages.

In this case, if Havitz volunteered to give up his seat, he was fully responsible for the cost of the rental car. Although his agency could not reimburse him for this expense, he was entitled to keep any compensation the airline provided him for giving up his seat.

The government is entitled to such benefits only if it pays the extra costs caused by the disrupted travel. If Havitz was involuntarily denied a seat on the plane, the airline would have been required to book him on another flight as soon as possible. Under such circumstances, if Havitz chose to rent a car instead of waiting for the next available flight, he would have been entitled to reimbursement up to the cost the government would have incurred for lodging and per diem as a result of the delayed travel.

201 Can an agency take any administrative action against a government traveler for voluntarily giving up an airline seat to obtain personal compensation from the airline?

Government employees are not expected to give up their reserved seat on a scheduled flight voluntarily if it will interfere with the performance of their official duties. For example, if a government traveler gives up his/her seat voluntarily and the rebooked flight is delayed, causing the traveler to miss work hours or a scheduled meeting, the traveler may be charged annual leave in accordance with FTR section 301-10.117.

202 The FTR states that travelers are required to use a government contractor–issued travel charge card for transportation but not specifically for lodging. Can a traveler use a personal credit card to earn lodging benefits since government travelers are allowed to retain promotional benefits?

No. FTR section 301-53.4 states in part that "you may not choose a travel service provider to gain frequent traveler benefits for personal use." Also, the FTR states that you are "required to use the government contractor–issued travel charge card for all official travel expenses unless you have an exemption" (section 301-51.1) and you are "required to use the government contractor–issued travel charge card for expenses directly related to your official travel" (section 301-51.6).

In addition, to ensure that travelers take advantage of certain government lodging agreements through agency or other government lodging agreements, FTR section 301-11.11 states in part that "when selecting a commercial lodging facility, first consideration should be given to government lodging agreement programs."

203 Can a traveler be reimbursed for an airline ticket obtained using frequent-flyer miles?

Travelers are reimbursed for actual expenses incurred. Because there is no statute or regulatory guidance on how to calculate the value of frequent flyer miles, airline tickets obtained through the use of frequent flyer miles are not reimbursable even for an emergency.

In CBCA 2470-TRAV, *In the Matter of Marc V. Dinger* (January 26, 2012), a civilian Army employee was stationed in Japan on March 11, 2011, when an earthquake and tsunami devastated the nation. In the aftermath, an evacuation order was issued, authorizing dependents of employees of the United States to voluntarily leave the island. The evacuation order provided for reimbursement of transportation expenses for travel that occurred between March 16 and April 15, 2011. Dinger's family elected to evacuate.

Dinger's family members used frequent flyer miles to obtain airline tickets and paid a surcharge of $145.80 in taxes and fees. They flew from Japan to Los Angeles on March 20, 2011.

After the travel was completed, Dinger contacted a representative of the Defense Finance and Accounting Service and asked whether he could be reimbursed for the use of frequent-flyer miles for air travel. The agency responded that he could not be reimbursed, so he submitted his travel voucher without requesting airfare reimbursement. Later, on June 27, 2011, Dinger filed a request for reimbursement with the CBCA.

The CBCA found that Dinger was entitled to reimbursement only for the actual expenses he incurred. As a general rule, authorized emergency travel is reimbursable. Under federal statute (5 U.S.C. 5725), the government can pay the transportation expenses of an employee's dependents to a safe haven location when an evacuation is authorized. JTR C6200 provides for the travel and transportation expenses for dependents of civilian employees authorized to depart the permanent duty station.

Reimbursement for purchases made with frequent flyer miles is another story, however. There is no statute or regulatory guidance on how to calculate the value of frequent flyer miles. As the board explained: “In the absence of specific statutory or regulatory guidance, it is not possible to conclude that an employee who redeemed frequent-flyer miles or a coupon to obtain a ticket for government travel actually incurred an expense, and it is not possible, with any certainty, to ascertain the amount of the expense.

The board acknowledged, however, that Dinger is entitled to reimbursement for the cost of actual expenses incurred—in this case, the $145.80 in taxes and fees—and directed the agency to reimburse Dinger that amount.

204 Can a traveler be reimbursed for the administrative fee that a car rental agency assesses as a part of the traveler’s participation in its travel incentive rewards program?

No. Any costs associated with an incentive rewards program are to be paid by the traveler. This fee is considered a personal expense and should not be reimbursed to the traveler.

205 Can a traveler be reimbursed for the cost of purchasing an official airline ticket using flight coupons received for personal use from an airline?

No. Travelers are reimbursed for actual expenses incurred related to official travel. The government is unable to ascertain the value of a flight coupon because no expense is incurred by a traveler using flight coupons to obtain an airline ticket for official travel.

In GSBCA 15636-TRAV, *In the Matter of Lawrence Baranski* (October 25, 2001), instead of purchasing his airfare for an official assignment with the federal travel charge card, Baranksi redeemed flight vouchers he had received from United Airlines for relinquishing his seat on a previous personal travel flight. He requested reimbursement of $361, the market value of the airfare.

The GSBCA found that he could not be reimbursed because he did not incur any expense. In addition, the board reasoned that permitting reimbursement would be problematic because of the:

- Substantial difficulty in ascertaining the value of the frequent flier miles or coupons
- Problems of control and accountability in allowing reimbursement for frequent flier miles and coupons
- Lack of guidance in statutes and regulations on how to value such items.

PART IX

Relocation

Relocation is a complex aspect of travel. The FTR requires agencies to establish policies on more than 50 separate issues; employees should refer to Part 302 of the FTR for detailed guidance and specific policy requirements pertaining to relocation and relocation allowances.

To ensure that relocation is in the best interest of the government, before authorizing a relocation allowance, agencies must have internal policies that determine:

- How the agency will implement the governing policies
- How the agency will determine when a relocation is in the best interest of the government
- When the agency will allow a travel advance for relocation expenses
- Who will authorize and approve relocation travel
- Under what additional circumstances the agency will require an employee to sign a service agreement.
- Who is required to sign a service agreement
- How the agency will ensure that all relocating employees sign a duplicate reimbursement disclosure statement, which is then incorporated into their relocation service agreements.

FTR Subchapter B—Relocation Allowances, Part 302-3—Relocation by Specific Type, provides 11 tables that detail exactly which benefits are mandatory and which are optional for each type of employee relocation (see Appendix B).

206 Should a relocating employee follow the FTR, GSA guidance, or agency policy?

Part 302 of the FTR is the controlling document regarding relocation. In addition, GSA has issued guidance documents based on established policies to assist employees regarding relocation and relocation allowances. Agency policy should be clear and should not conflict with Part 302 of the FTR under any circumstances. In the case of a discrepancy, Part 302 of the FTR takes precedence over any guidance document issued by GSA or any policy document issued by an agency.

For example, in CBCA 943-RELO, *In the Matter of William P. McBee, Jr., and Judith L. Sammel* (January 3, 2008), two National Security Agency (NSA) employees who are married to each other were transferred to a permanent duty station in Europe. In securing a permanent residence, the couple encountered a vast array of conflicting policies and procedures regarding their temporary quarters subsistence allowance (TQSA).

McBee and Sammel both reported for duty in Europe on July 7. NSA had assigned to them a permanent change of station sponsor, who advised that because housing in the area was "a real pain," they should expect to spend about 60 days in temporary quarters before finding permanent housing. Following this advice, they signed an eight-week lease on an apartment, where they stayed from July 7 to September 1.

To locate a permanent residence, McBee and Sammel were told to use the services of an NSA housing officer. Beginning on July 18, the officer showed them three houses, two of which had inadequate parking facilities and one of which was rented by someone else immediately after they saw it. On July 24, the couple began searching on their own and found an apartment on August 1. Unfortunately, they could not sign a lease until the housing officer approved it, and he refused to sign the lease because he had not been involved in finding the apartment. Finally, on August 10, he approved the apartment. The couple then arranged to move in on September 1 to allow the landlord time to provide necessary carpet replacement and repainting. In total, the couple stayed in temporary quarters for 55 days.

Meanwhile, the couple had attempted, in vain, to determine the length of time they were eligible for TQSA. A summary of permanent change of station entitlements given to Sammel indicated that they were entitled to TQSA for the first 45 days.

However, a desk officer explained that the standard NSA allowance is up to 45 days, but can be extended for circumstances beyond the employee's control. NSA documents were equally conflicting. A July 2003 housing directive from the NSA Europe office provides that employees are limited to 45 days TQSA "with the possibility of up to 10 additional days in certain situations." A summer 2005 NSA publication called *Global HR Post-its* authorizes an initial 45 days of TQSA, not to exceed 60 days. The list goes on.

The couple requested TQSA for a period of 55 days. NSA reimbursed them for 45 days but refused to make payment for the additional 10 days. The couple appealed to the CBCA.

The CBCA summed up the situation: Going from most to least restrictive versions, the NSA policy might be 30 days, with a possible extension of 15 days; 45 days; 45 days, with a possible extension of 10 days; 45 days, with a possible extension of 15 days; 45 days, with a possible extension of unspecified length; and 45 days, with a possible extension of 75 days.

In reviewing the case, the CBCA attempted to determine the specifics of NSA's TQSA policy. Under the Overseas Differentials and Allowances Act, agencies may pay employees who are stationed abroad a TQSA of 90 days or less "after the first arrival at a new post of assignment in a foreign area or a period ending with the occupation of residence quarters, whichever is shorter." 5 U.S.C. 5923(a)(1)(A)(2000). The period may be extended for 60 additional days if the head of the agency determines that the employee continues to occupy temporary quarters due to compelling reasons beyond his/her control.

Sections 121 and 122.2 of the Department of State Standardized Regulations (DSSR) restate the time limitations provided in the Overseas Differentials and Allowances Act. However, Section 122.3 provides that "an agency or post may . . . limit the number of days TQSA may be paid to fewer than the maximum number of days."

The CBCA acknowledged that Section 122.3 authorized NSA to limit its TQSA policy. However, it found that NSA had not, in fact, created a uniform policy limiting TQSA. Furthermore, any policy that would allow posts the discretion to limit the number of days on an employee-by-employee basis without prescribed standards would be "manifestly unfair."

The CBCA took NSA to task for the confusion surrounding its TQSA policy: "NSA has failed miserably at the task of establishing a limitation on the number of days of TQSA eligibility through a clear policy." It determined that neither NSA nor the post to which McBee and Sammel had been assigned had a policy limiting the number of days an employee is eligible for TQSA. Consequently, sections 121 and 122.2 of the DSSR, which prescribed eligibility for 90 days, with a possible extension of 60 days, applied. McBee and Sammel were therefore entitled to TQSA reimbursement for all 55 days.

The CBCA noted that even if NSA had a policy similar to what had been explained to the couple before they left—45 days, with a possible extension of unspecified length—it still would have approved their claim. The couple had acted promptly and responsibly in finding permanent quarters; meanwhile, the agency was dilatory, particularly due to the housing officer's delay in approving the lease for the apartment the couple had located.

207 Has GSA issued a policy guide for relocation?

Yes. During 2011, GSA issued three relocation policy guides: (1) *Relocation Policy Guide for Federal Civilian Agencies*, (2) *Handbook for Relocating Federal Employees*, and (3) *Glossary of Acronyms and Terms for Federal Civilian Relocation*.

208 Can those documents be considered regulatory or mandatory for managing an agency's relocation program?

No. The GSA documents are guidance documents based on established policies, but the FTR is the controlling source for rules governing federal civilian relocations. Employees should use guidance documents as a reference guide to supplement the FTR and gain a better understanding of relocation rules and procedures.

209 Why would GSA develop relocation guides instead of just referring agencies to Part 302 of the FTR?

GSA developed the guides to help:

- Executives understand the basic issues involved in relocation policy
- Relocation managers develop their agency-level relocation policies
- Program managers determine whether to offer relocation and to select the relocation benefits they will include.

210 What other resources does GSA provide to assist employees with relocations?

GSA has aggregated information from federal agencies that offer relocation services to other federal agencies on a fee-for-service basis. Referred to as relocation resource centers (RRCs), these agencies offer permanent change of station services in the areas of home sale, household goods, storage, employee counseling, and taxes. The following agencies have voluntarily nominated themselves as RRCs:

- Department of Health and Human Services
- Department of Interior
- Department of Treasury, Bureau of the Public Debt
- Department of Veterans Affairs
- Environmental Protection Agency
- General Services Administration, Federal Acquisition Service.

For more detailed information about relocation services provided by a specific RRC and contact information, visit the GSA website at www.gsa.gov under Relocation Resource Centers.

211 Are the relocation resource centers endorsed by GSA?

No. The federal agencies and programs listed above and on the GSA website have voluntarily nominated themselves as RRCs. Neither GSA nor its Office of Governmentwide Policy (OGP) endorses any single center or group of centers. Additionally, OGP's Office of

Travel, Transportation and Asset Management does not substantiate any of the claims or statements made by the agencies concerning their center's PCS service offerings.

212 What are the guiding principles for federal relocation managers?

GSA promulgates the following ten principles for federal relocation managers:

1. Relocation must be in the interest of the government; it should actively support the agency's mission and it may not be allowed primarily for the convenience of the transferee.
2. Relocation should be authorized and managed in a manner consistent with the agency's human capital strategic plan.
3. Relocation should be planned as far in advance as possible.
4. Relocation should be managed through a comprehensive automated relocation management system.
5. When developing a job announcement that will include relocation, the agency should determine:
   - The relationship between the agency mission, the job announcement, and the need to offer relocation
   - Which optional relocation benefits will be offered
   - The estimated cost.
6. No policy can (or is intended to) cover all the expenses or remove all the inconveniences that might be involved in a relocation.
7. Not all relocation allowances are entitlements. The discretionary benefits should be provided only when they advance the interest of the government.
8. Agencies should make every reasonable effort to limit the stress of relocation on transferees and their families.
9. Personal and financial information about the transferee and his/her family must be safeguarded.
10. Transferees are expected to make every reasonable effort to take an active role in managing their relocations, with the dual goals of minimizing overall cost to the government and becoming productive in their new jobs as quickly as possible.

213 Who is eligible for relocation allowances?

An employee is generally eligible for relocation expense allowances in accordance with the FTR if he/she is:

- A new appointee appointed to his/her first official station
- An employee transferring in the interest of the government from one agency or duty station to another for permanent duty, and the new duty station is at least 50 miles distant from the old duty station
- An employee of the United States Postal Service transferred for permanent duty, under 39 U.S.C. 1006, from the Postal Service to an agency as defined in 5 U.S.C. 5721
- An employee performing travel in accordance with an overseas tour renewal agreement
- An employee returning to his/her place of residence after completion of a prescribed tour of duty for the purposes of separation from government service or separation from the overseas assignment for reassignment to the same or different government agency
- A student trainee assigned to any position upon completion of college work
- An employee eligible for a "last move home" benefit upon separation from the government (and the immediate family in the event of the employee's death prior to separation or after separation but prior to relocating)
- A Department of Defense overseas dependents school system teacher
- A career appointee to the Senior Executive Service (SES) as defined in 5 U.S.C. 3132(a)(4), and a prior SES appointee who is returning to his/her official residence for separation and who will be retaining SES retirement benefits
- An employee who is being assigned to a temporary duty station in connection with a long-term assignment.

214 Are any individuals not eligible for relocation allowances?

The following individuals are not eligible to receive relocation expense allowances:

- A foreign service officer or a federal employee transferred under the rules of the Foreign Service Act of 1980, as amended
- An officer or an employee transferred under the Central Intelligence Act of 1949, as amended
- A person whose pay and allowances are prescribed under title 37 U.S.C., Pay and Allowances of the Uniformed Services
- An employee of the Department of Veterans Affairs to whom 38 U.S.C. 235 applies
- A person not covered in question #213.

215 What are the types of relocations?

There are two types of relocations:

- *Permanent change of station* (PCS) – an assignment of a new appointee to an official station or the transfer of an employee from one official station to another on a permanent basis
- *Temporary change of station* (TCS) – the relocation to a new official station for a temporary period while performing a long-term assignment, and subsequent return to the previous official station upon completion of that assignment.

216 What types of employees can be relocated?

New appointees and transferred employees can be relocated.

217 Are all types of relocation expenses reimbursable?

No. There are mandatory and discretionary relocation allowances. See FTR Subchapter B – Relocation Allowances Part 302-3 Relocation by Specific Type and Appendix B in this guidebook.

218 What is a new appointee?

A new appointee is:

- An individual who is employed with the federal government for the very first time (including an individual who has performed transition activities under section 3 of the Presidential Transition Act of 1963 (3 U.S.C. 102 note), and is appointed in the same fiscal year as the Presidential inauguration)
- An employee who is returning to the government after a break in service (except an employee separated as a result of a reduction in force or a transfer of functions who is re-employed within one year after such action)
- A student trainee assigned to the government upon completion of his/her college work.

It is important for new appointees to know their relocation entitlements, which differ from relocation entitlements for transferees.

In CBCA 228-RELO, *In the Matter of Rafael E. Arroyo* (July 11, 2011), the Food and Drug Administration (FDA) hired a new employee in January 2009. Since January 2010, Arroyo had been trying to rent or sell his home in Puerto Rico and rent or purchase a home in Maryland. He sought additional time and eligibility to receive relocation benefits for accomplishing these tasks, which the FDA denied. Arroyo appealed to the CBCA, which denied his claim.

The CBCA determined that Arroyo was not eligible for those benefits. In its decision, the board outlined the new-hire provisions contained in sections 5722 and 5723 of the U.S. Code. Generally, agencies may authorize reimbursement for the travel and transportation of a new hire and his/her immediate family, the transportation and temporary storage of household goods, and the cost of shipping a POV from the place of residence at the time of hire to the first duty station. 5 U.S.C. 5723 (2006). Agencies may not provide new employees with reimbursement of expenses associated with the sale of residences at old locations or the purchase of new ones at the initial duty station. "Those benefits," the board noted, "are provided only to employees who are transferred in the interest of the government." 5 U.S.C. 5742(d).

219 What is a transferee or transferred employee?

A transferred employee is an employee who transfers from one official station to another. This may also include employees separated as a result of a reduction in force or a transfer of functions who are re-employed within one year after such separation.

220 What are the types of transfers?

There are five types of transfers:

- Relocation of two or more employed immediate family members
- Reduction-in-force
- Overseas assignment and return
- Overseas tour renewal
- Prior return of immediate family members.

221 What are the types of separation relocations?

There are two types of separation relocations: overseas to U.S. return separation and SES separation for retirement.

For overseas to U.S. return separation, employees should be fully aware of the consequences, including financial liabilities, of deciding to separate while overseas without returning to the United States as authorized.

A good example is CBCA 1707-TRAV, *In the Matter of Michael W. Silva* (January 12, 2010). In the case, a budget officer with the U.S. Marine Corps transferred from Orlando, Florida, to work at the Marine Corps Air Station in Iwakuni, Japan. After working for more than three years at the air station, Silva left government service and took a job as a minister and senior pastor at the Calvary Chapel, near Iwakuni.

As Silva's work at the Marine Corps Air Station was coming to an end, the agency's Civilian Human Resource Office (CHRO) issued travel orders stating that he was returning to his "actual residence" of Orlando. The next day, the CHRO amended the orders to state that

Silva's "new official station and location, actual residence, or alternate destination" was an off-base address in Iwakuni. The office issued the travel orders because, as a separating employee remaining abroad, Silva was entitled to allowable expenses in relocating to Iwakuni, including shipment of household goods (HHG). The CHRO explained that it issued the amended travel orders because the Travel Management Office would not otherwise allow Silva to move his HHG to Iwakuni.

It was not disputed that Silva was entitled to shipment of HHG per his permanent relocation to Iwakuni. However, Silva believed that he was also entitled to a return trip to Orlando under the service agreement that he had signed when he initially moved to Iwakuni with the Marine Corps.

About two weeks after accepting a job with the Calvary Chapel, Silva and his family flew to Orlando from Hiroshima, Japan. They stayed in Orlando for close to a month and then returned to Japan. The travel voucher he submitted for reimbursement of one-way fares for himself and his family was rejected by the Marine Corps finance office on the basis that Orlando was not his actual residence. Silva appealed the decision to the CBCA.

The board emphasized that agencies may pay travel and transportation expenses of employees who return from overseas posts to which they were transferred. The board then looked to federal travel regulations to determine whether Silva's permanent relocation to Iwakuni negated his travel entitlement.

The JTR (sections C5085-A and C5085-B) provides for separation travel from OCONUS duty. JTR section C5085-B provides:

"An employee is:

1. Authorized travel and transportation allowances for travel from the OCONUS PDS to the actual residence established at the time of appointment/transfer to the OCONUS PDS
2. Authorized travel and transportation allowances for travel to an alternate destination NTE [not to exceed] the constructed cost for travel from the OCONUS PDS to the actual residence
3. Personally financially responsible for any excess costs
4. Not authorized travel and transportation allowances if separated from a PDS in the same locality as the actual residence/alternate location."

In sum, the JTR provides transportation and HHG shipment benefits to the place where the employee relocates after separation from an overseas station. If Silva had relocated back to Orlando when he separated from the Marine Corps, he would have been entitled to reimbursement of allowable travel and shipment of HHG expenses.

Since he chose to remain abroad after separation, he was entitled only to the allowable expenses in relocating to Iwakuni, not to exceed what it would have cost to relocate to Orlando—which he received. The board denied Silva's claim.

222 What determines an employee's entitlements and allowances for relocation?

Entitlements and allowances for relocation are determined by the regulatory provisions in effect at the time the employee reports for duty at the new official station. However, this does not change the requirement that all aspects of a relocation must be completed in the timeframes specified in the FTR.

223 What are the mandatory and discretionary benefits?

Subchapter B – Relocation Allowances Part 302-3 Relocation by Specific Type of the FTR provides 11 tables (see Appendix B of this guidebook) that detail exactly which benefits are mandatory and which are optional for each type of employee relocation. The following is a simplified list of allowances that are optional in most cases:

- Househunting trips
- TQSE
- Shipment of POVs
- Use of a relocation services center
- Property management services
- Home marketing incentives.

224 What are the mandatory elements under the FTR for most relocations?

Once an agency authorizes a relocation expense under the terms and conditions of the FTR, the following must be paid:

- Service agreements
- Transportation and per diem for the transferee and immediate family
- Transportation of household goods
- Temporary storage of household goods
- Extended storage of household goods
- Mobile homes that are used as a primary residence
- Residence transactions
- Miscellaneous expenses
- Taxes on relocation expenses.

225 What is a service agreement?

A service agreement is a written agreement between the employee and the agency, signed by the employee and an agency representative, stating that the employee will remain in the service of the government for a period of time as specified in the FTR (section 302-2.13) after the employee has relocated. A service agreement must also include the duplicate reimbursement disclosure statement specified in the FTR (sections 302-2.22, 302-2.23, and 302-2.100(g)).

226 What is a duplicate reimbursement disclosure statement?

A duplicate reimbursement disclosure statement is a written statement signed by the employee and submitted to the agency. It states that the employee and his/her immediate family have not accepted, and will not accept, duplicate reimbursement for relocation expenses. Furthermore, it states that, to the best of the employee's knowledge, no third party has accepted duplicate reimbursement for the employee's relocation expenses. The duplicate reimbursement disclosure statement must be incorporated into the employee's service agreement.

The employee must sign a duplicate reimbursement disclosure statement to receive any relocation benefits.

227 When is a service agreement required?

A service agreement is required if the employee is receiving reimbursement for relocation travel expenses.

228 When is a service agreement not needed or required?

A service agreement is not needed for a temporary change of station (TCS). Nor is a service agreement required for an SES employee's last move home. In addition, a new service agreement is not required for an employee who is returning from a destination outside the continental United States, on the return portion of his/her original orders, when the new authorization is only for shipment of household goods, privately owned vehicles, and transportation of the transferee and family.

229 How long is a service agreement?

Service agreements can range in length from 12 to 36 months, depending on agency policy and whether the relocation is within or outside the continental United States (CONUS or OCONUS).

230 Is an employee required to sign a service agreement when transferring within or outside the continental United States or performing renewal agreement travel? What is the minimum period of service?

Yes, the employee is required to sign a service agreement when transferring within or outside the continental United States or performing renewal agreement travel. The minimum periods of service are:

- Within the continental United States for a period of service of not less than 12 months following the effective date of transfer
- Outside the continental United States for an agreed-upon period of service of not more than 36 months or less than 12 months following the effective date of transfer
- Department of Defense Overseas Dependent School System teachers for a period of not less than one school year as determined under chapter 25 of Title 20, U.S. Code
- For renewal agreement travel a period of not less than 12 months from the date of return to the same or different overseas official station.

231 Can an employee be penalized for violating a service agreement?

Yes. If an employee violates a service agreement (other than for reasons beyond the employee's control and which must be accepted by the agency), the employee will have incurred a debt due to the government and must reimburse all costs that the agency has paid toward the employee's relocation expenses, including the withholding tax allowance and relocation income tax allowance. It is within an agency's discretion to determine whether, under the particular circumstances, to include a separation from service as a reason beyond an employee's control and acceptable to the agency.

In CBCA 1433-RELO. *In the Matter of David F. Lytal* (February 27, 2009), in the spring of 2005, David Lytal began a three-year tour of duty as the Director of the Drug Enforcement Agency (DEA) International Law Enforcement Academy in Bangkok, Thailand. In October 2007, he requested an early departure from his tour. He asked to be relocated to the United States, indicating that his son was ill and that he was needed back in the United States to take care of him. The DEA's Career Board approved Lytal's request and reassigned him to DEA headquarters in Washington, D.C.

On November 5, 2007, before Lytal had agreed to the relocation to Washington, D.C., he informed the agency's Transportation Management Unit that he would be retiring soon after returning to the United States. He was advised that the relocation was conditional upon his signing a DEA 114 Service Agreement – Domestic Transfer form, in which he would agree to remain employed with the federal government for 12 months. Lytal was also advised that if he left the federal government before the 12 months was up, he would be required to reimburse the government for some of the costs of his PCS move.

Ten days later, on November 15, Lytal reiterated to the Transportation Management Unit that he planned to retire upon his return to the United States. He was told that unless his return travel was for the purpose of separating from the service, he needed to sign a DEA 114, agreeing to remain in government service for at least 12 months.

On November 21, 2007, Lytal signed the DEA 114 service agreement, agreeing to remain employed by the government for at least 12 months or repay the government for the cost of his relocation. He then retired from federal service about seven months later, in June 2008.

The DEA asked Lytal to repay $3,734.28 in travel expenses, representing his return to the United States. Lytal, believing that it was unfair that he was required to repay his travel expenses, appealed to the CBCA.

The CBCA confirmed that the DEA was correct in requiring Lytal to repay the travel expenses. FTR section 302-2.13 states that reimbursement for relocation costs is conditional upon an employee's entering into a 12-month service agreement. Section 302-2.14 further provides: "If you violate a service agreement (other than for reasons beyond your control and which must be accepted by your agency), you will have incurred a debt due to the government and you must reimburse all costs that your agency has paid towards your relocation expenses."

It is possible that Lytal could have sought relief from having to repay the travel expenses on the grounds that he left the service agreement for reasons beyond his control—to care for his son. However, he did not assert that his separation was for a reason beyond his control. Lytal also could have simply retired before returning to the United States. He was advised by the DEA that he would be entitled to benefits if he retired while at a foreign post of duty. The benefits, however, differed from the ones he would be entitled to under a permanent change of station move.

Lytal claimed to the CBCA that he refused to sign the service agreement until he was advised that the DEA usually does not request reimbursement of travel costs in situations where an employee breaks a service agreement. The DEA vehemently denied this claim. However, even if he had received that advice, it would not have affected his case: The CBCA has consistently and repeatedly found that mistaken advice is not grounds for allowing a claim. Instead, federal employees are expected to know and understand the rules of relocation and travel.

The CBCA summed it up: "When claimant resigned from federal service he was well aware of the requirements of the separation agreement . . . . Apparently, claimant simply took the chance that the DEA would not enforce the agreement. He lost that gamble."

The CBCA determined that the DEA was reasonable in requiring Lytal to repay the $3,734.28.

232 When is a decision beyond the employee's control for an employee to break a service agreement?

Although agencies have discretion to determine whether a reason is beyond an employee's control and is acceptable, the CBCA's role in such matters is to decide whether the agency's determination has a reasonable basis. The CBCA has made several decisions in which an employee's reason for breaking a service agreement was determined to be personal, including resignations and retirement; the CBCA upheld the agency's determination that these reasons were unacceptable.

For example, in CBCA 460-RELO, *In the Matter of Marilyn Fournier* (February 21, 2007), an Air Force employee was transferred to New Orleans. As part of the transfer, Fournier signed a service agreement promising 12 months of government service in return for the government's payment of her relocation costs. The agreement provided that if she separated from the government before completing the 12-month agreement, she would have to repay the relocation reimbursement—unless she separated for reasons beyond her control that were acceptable to the agency.

After her transfer to New Orleans, Fournier's husband was unable to find a suitable job in the area. He instead accepted a job at Kirtland Air Force Base, New Mexico. Four months after her transfer, Fournier left her position in New Orleans to be with her husband in New Mexico. Although she initially looked for another job with the government, she ultimately accepted a job with an Air Force contractor. Five months after that, she was rehired by the government. The Air Force asked Fournier to repay the relocation reimbursement it had provided for her transfer to New Orleans because she had left government service just four months later.

Unsure whether the Air Force had acted correctly, Fournier appealed to the CBCA. She argued that her husband's relocation caused her to separate from the government for a reason beyond her control that should have been acceptable to the agency.

The CBCA disagreed. It noted that agencies have discretion to determine whether a reason is beyond an employee's control and acceptable to the agency; the board's only role is to decide whether the agency's determination has a reasonable basis. Furthermore, the board had previously found, in GSBCA 14724-RELO, *In the Matter of John A. Bukowski* (1998), that an employee's resignation in order to accompany a transferred spouse was not a separation beyond the employee's control. The board found that Fournier's decision to quit her job to accompany her spouse was ultimately a personal choice. Therefore, it was reasonable for the Air Force to determine that her reason for resigning was neither beyond her control nor acceptable to the agency.

Fournier also asked the board to determine whether her work for a federal contractor could be considered a continuation of "government service" under her service agreement. She had, after all, provided service to the government, albeit under contract. The CBCA said no: A contractor who performs services for the government is not in government service for the purpose of complying with a service agreement.

Interestingly, the CBCA noted that service agreements require the employee only to stay in the service of the government, not in the service of a specific agency. If Fournier had found a position with another government agency, she might have been able to complete her service agreement and possibly keep her relocation reimbursement.

233 What happens if an employee fails to sign a service agreement?

If an employee fails to sign a service agreement, the agency will not pay relocation expenses.

234 Can a service agreement be voided by a subsequent service agreement?

No. Service agreements that are already in effect cannot be voided by subsequent service agreements.

235 If an employee has more than one service agreement, is the employee required to adhere to each agreement separately?

Yes. Service agreements cannot be grouped together and must be adhered to separately. Each agreement is in effect for the period specified in the agreement.

236 Can relocation expenses be paid if allowed in the agency's policy but not in the vacancy announcement?

To qualify for relocation benefits, the vacancy announcement must have addressed whether or not relocation benefits will be provided. Relocation is not something that can be decided or negotiated after the employee has accepted the new position.

In CBCA 526-RELO, *In the Matter of Gary L. Dissette* (May 3, 2007), a civilian employee of the Army transferred in June 2000 from the Crane Army Ammunition Activity in Indiana to a position in Germany with the Army Audit Agency. The employee had return rights to the Crane base.

In 2004, Dissette prepared to return to Crane. He was entitled to reimbursement for air travel for him and his family, as well as transportation of household goods. His orders did not authorize real estate expenses or a miscellaneous expense allowance.

While planning his return to Crane, Dissette also applied for a position as an accountant for the U.S. Army Field Support Command in Rock Island, Illinois. The vacancy announcement for the position stated that "permanent change of station (PCS) expenses are not authorized."

At the time, paragraph C5010 of the JTR offered guidelines that seemed tailormade to Dissette's situation. Under the provision, an employee relocating from an overseas assignment to an official duty station within the continental United States other than the duty station from which he/she had originally been transferred overseas was entitled to reimbursement of real estate transaction expenses and a miscellaneous expense allowance.

Dissette wondered whether taking the position in Rock Island would net him reimbursement of real estate transaction expenses and a miscellaneous expense allowance, as provided by the JTR. He believed that because such reimbursement was authorized in the JTR, it was a mandatory entitlement that superseded the job announcement's statement that PCS expenses would not be paid. When Dissette asked Rock Island personnel if he would be eligible for reimbursement, he was told that he "had a choice to make—take the job or not."

Dissette took the job in Rock Island. Upon arriving at his new official duty station, he once again brought up the issue of reimbursement for real estate transaction expenses and a miscellaneous expense allowance. His command advised him that he was not eligible for reimbursement, but recommended that he try to submit a voucher to the Defense Finance and Accounting Service (DFAS). DFAS rejected his claim, stating that he could not be reimbursed based on the terms of the vacancy announcement.

Dissette then asked the CBCA to review the matter. The board found that DFAS was right: The agency could not reimburse his relocation claim because the vacancy announcement did not authorize PCS expenses.

The CBCA explained that under the JTR provision, the expenses and allowances are payable when "it is in the government's interest" to transfer an employee from one official duty station to another. The board had previously found that one of the ways an agency may communicate its determination that a transfer is not considered in the government's interest is by specifying in the vacancy announcement that relocation benefits will not be provided.

In this case, the decision not to pay relocation benefits for the Rock Island position was clearly communicated in the job posting. Therefore, the transfer was not considered in the government's interest. The board denied Dissette's claim.

237 May an employee be reimbursed for relocation expenses if relocation to a new official station does not meet the 50-mile distance test?

Generally no; employees may not be reimbursed for relocation expenses if they relocate to a new official station that does not meet the 50-mile distance test as stated in FTR section 302-2.6:

"(a) The distance test is met when the new official station is at least 50 miles further from the employee's current residence than the old official station is from the same residence. For example, if the old official station is 3 miles from the current residence, then the new official station must be at least 53 miles from that same residence in order to receive relocation expenses for residence transactions. The distance between the official station and residence is the shortest of the commonly traveled routes between them. The distance test does not take into consideration the location of a new residence. This follows the distance guidelines found in *Internal Revenue Service Publication 521, Moving Expenses*.

(b) The head of your agency or designee may authorize an exception to the 50-mile threshold on a case-by-case basis when he/she determines that it is in the best interest of the government. However, the agency cannot waive the applicability of the Internal Revenue Service that is, all reimbursed expenses would be taxable income to you, and the agency would have to reimburse those taxes.

(c) Any relocation must be incidental to the transfer and not for the convenience of the employee."

238 Can an employee rely on the shipper's estimate?

No. The accepted practice is to use the "certified weight" as the measure of the actual tonnage transported.

In GSBCA 16744-RELO, *In the Matter of Steven W. Anderson* (Jan. 19, 2006), an employee of the Department of the Interior's Bureau of Land Management (BLM) was authorized a permanent change of station. BLM determined that the transfer was in the best interest of the government and approved Anderson for relocation benefits.

Anderson owned a home at his old duty station, so BLM arranged a moving company to ship his household goods (HHG) to his new location. As a first step in that process, the moving company contacted Anderson and arranged a time to inspect the HHG to be transported. The company arrived at Anderson's home as agreed and inspected his HHG. It estimated the HHG's total weight at 17,172 pounds.

Based on the company's estimate, Anderson believed that the shipment of his HHG would be fully reimbursed by BLM. Unfortunately, after the goods had been loaded for transportation by the moving company and weighed by a certified truck scale, the actual weight was 18,900 pounds. The company submitted an invoice to BLM for its services based on the certified tonnage.

Section 302-7.2 of the FTR authorizes agencies to pay the shipment of employees' HHG up to 18,000 pounds; accordingly, BLM determined that Anderson should pay the costs of shipping the additional 900 pounds. Anderson appealed to the GSBCA, arguing that he should not have to pay the excess charges because he relied on the mover's original estimate.

The board found that BLM acted correctly in seeking payment from Anderson. It emphasized that agencies may pay the costs of moving goods only up to 18,000 pounds. While the board recognized that Anderson relied on the mover's original estimate, it noted that the accepted practice is to use the certified weight as the measure of the actual tonnage transported. Accordingly, BLM was prohibited from paying the expense of moving the additional 900 pounds.

239 Can an agency encourage an employee to relocate in order to fulfill an agency-specific mission and later reimburse the employee for relocation expenses?

The number one guiding principle for federal relocation managers is that relocation must be in the interest of the government; it should actively support the agency's mission, and it may not be allowed primarily for the convenience of the transferee.

In GSBCA 16832-RELO, *In the Matter of Lindell Baker* (Aug. 3, 2006), the United States Geological Survey (USGS) announced to its employees its strategy to implement a new program called the National Map. In support of the initiative, USGS encouraged employees to voluntarily relocate to "priority areas." The agency, however, made clear that relocation would be the "employee's choice" and that "travel, transportation, and relocation expenses would be the responsibility of the employee."

Forty-three employees initially showed interest in voluntarily relocating. Fifteen eventually did, including Lindell Baker. Baker relocated from Denver, Colorado, to Bozeman, Montana. As part of his transfer, Baker signed a statement that provided: "I voluntarily request consideration for assignment to a position in another commuting area. I am making this request primarily for my personal convenience or benefit. I understand that, if selected, I will be responsible for all travel, transportation, and relocation expenses associated with reporting for duty in that position."

Approximately three years after Baker's relocation, USGS announced that employees supporting the National Map initiative would be downsized by competitive sourcing. As a result, many employees would lose their jobs. The agency determined that the program would be located in Denver and only those employees in the Denver commuting area would be eligible to compete for remaining positions.

Unhappy that he had transferred from Denver at USGS's encouragement and now could not compete for a job, Baker contacted his congressman. He asserted that he had been treated "unfairly, since he [would] lose his job due to the reorganization . . . and would be out of pocket approximately $10,000 in relocation costs." He also noted that he "volunteered" to move to Montana because USGS had represented that those who relocated would have a "much more secure future" with the agency.

It is unclear whether Baker's congressman contacted USGS for a response to his allegations. However, after Baker's communication with his congressional representative, the agency requested an opinion from the GSBCA regarding whether it could reimburse the relocation costs of the employees who had voluntarily relocated to support the National Map effort.

The board found that USGS could not pay those expenses. It made clear that agencies are authorized to pay an employee's moving expenses only if he/she is "transferred in the interests of the government." 5 U.S.C. 5724(a). When a "transfer is made primarily for the convenience or the benefit of an employee . . . or at his request, his expense . . . may not be allowed or paid from government funds." 5 U.S.C. 5724(h).

According to the GSBCA, an agency has wide discretion in determining whether a relocation is for an employee's "convenience" or in the "government's interest." Moreover, the board emphasized that it will not reverse such a decision unless it was arbitrary, capricious, or clearly erroneous; in this situation, that was not the case.

The board emphasized that the employees who relocated had each signed a statement that their move was primarily for their convenience or benefit. In addition, they agreed to be responsible for their relocation costs. Thus, USGS's determination that the employees' transfers were not in the interest of the government was reasonable and therefore proper.

240 Can an agency revoke relocation allowances verbally?

Although agencies have discretion to determine when relocation benefits should be paid, such discretion must be exercised in a fair and reasonable manner. The offer and revocation of relocation benefits must be provided in writing. Revocation of relocation benefits should be provided through the same vehicle used to make the offer initially to demonstrate that such action was taken in a fair and equitable manner. Otherwise, agencies risk reimbursing expenses they did not intend to pay.

In GSBA 16953-RELO, *In the Matter of Cecelia R. Williams* (Oct. 20, 2006), in March 2004, the Department of Veterans Affairs (VA) issued two vacancy announcements for an accountant position at the agency's central office in Washington, D.C. One announcement, posted internally, provided that relocation expenses were not authorized. The other announcement, posted on the USAJOBS website, opened the competition to applicants from other federal agencies and provided that relocation expenses were authorized. Both announcements specified that the selected individual would be at a level between a GS-9 and a GS-13.

Cecelia Williams, a GS-12 accountant with the Department of the Treasury in Parkersburg, West Virginia, applied for the position based on the USAJOBS posting. The VA selected her for an interview. During that process, she was advised by the VA that the USAJOB's notice regarding the payment of relocation expenses was incorrect.

Shortly after her interview, the VA offered Williams the position at the pay grade of a GS-13. She accepted and relocated to Washington, D.C. After starting work, Williams submitted a request for reimbursement of her moving costs. The VA refused to pay her expenses, so she appealed to the GSBCA.

The board found that Williams was entitled to reimbursement. It noted that the vacancy announcement posted on USAJOBS provided that the moving costs of an externally hired individual would be paid. The board found it immaterial that Williams was told in her interview that she would not be entitled to relocation expenses.

The GSBCA explained that the "selection of an employee pursuant to a merit promotion program is generally deemed to be an action taken in the interests of the government and therefore one for which relocation benefits will be paid." According to the board, this rule applies unless the agency:

- Determines that the transfer will primarily be for the benefit of the employee and that relocation benefits will therefore not be paid
- Communicates this finding in advance and in writing to all applicants.

In this case, the VA did not advise Williams (and *all* other applicants) in writing prior to offering her the promotion that her transfer costs would not be paid. In fact, the reverse was true: The written vacancy announcement provided that such expenses would be reimbursed. The GSBCA found that the oral notice provided to Williams during her interview was insufficient to revoke the agency's written determination in the USAJOBS posting.

APPENDIX A

References and Websites

These websites provide valuable information that may assist you as you plan and travel on government funds for official government business.

Federal Travel Regulation
http://www.gsa.gov/portal/content/104790

GSA Per Diem Rates
http://www.gsa.gov/portal/category/21287

POV Reimbursable Rates
http://www.gsa.gov/portal/content/100715

FedRooms
https://www.fedrooms.com

Civilian Board of Contract Appeals
http://www.cbca.gsa.gov

JFTR/JTR
http://www.defensetravel.dod.mil/site/travelreg.cfm

U.S. Government Rental Car and Truck Programs
http://www.defensetravel.dod.mil/site/rental.cfm

GSA Airline City Pair Search Tool
http://apps.fss.gsa.gov/citypairs/search

GSA SmartPay (includes state tax exempt forms, travel charge card)
https://smartpay.gsa.gov/about-gsa-smartpay/tax-information/state-response-letter

OMB Circular A-123, Appendix B
http://www.whitehouse.gov/sites/default/files/omb/circulars/a123/a123_appendix_b.pdf

Travel Card Program Guide for A/OPCs
https://smartpay.gsa.gov/sites/default/files/pub/5-11-00393%20SmartPay_Travel_%20AOPC_Guide%20_508.pdf

GSA Travel Reporting
http://www.gsa.gov/portal/category/27107

Alaska, Hawaii, Puerto Rico and U.S. Possessions Per Diem Rates
http://www.defensetravel.dod.mil/site/perdiemCalc.cfm

Foreign Per Diem Rates
http://aoprals.state.gov/content.asp?content_id=184&menu_id=78

Hotel-Motel Fire Safety Master List
http://apps.usfa.fema.gov/hotel/

Find a County for Per Diem
http://www.naco.org/Counties/Pages/FindACounty.aspx

M&IE Breakdown
http://www.gsa.gov/portal/content/101518

GAO Principles of Appropriations Law
http://www.gao.gov/legal/redbook/redbook.html

GAO Legal (Comptroller General and "B") Decisions
http://www.gao.gov/legal/index.html

GPO Official Printing of Government Documents
http://www.gpo.gov/fdsys/search/home.action

APPENDIX B

Relocation Tables

New Appointee

Table A: Assigned to First Official Station in the Continental United States (CONUS)

Column 1— Relocation allowances that agency must pay or reimburse	Column 2— Relocation allowances that agency has discretionary authority to pay or reimburse
(1) Transportation of employee & immediate family member(s) (Part 302-4 of this chapter).	(1) Shipment of privately owned vehicle (POV) (Subpart B of Part 302-9 of this chapter).
(2) Per diem for employee only (Part 302-4 of this chapter).	
(3) Transportation & temporary storage of household goods (Part 302-7 of this chapter).	
(4) Extended storage of household goods (Part 302-8 of this chapter).[1]	
(5) Transportation of a mobile home or boat used as a primary residence in lieu of the transportation of household goods (Part 302-10 of this chapter).	

[1]**Note to Column 1, Item 4:** Only when assigned to a designated isolated official station in CONUS.

Source: Feferal Travel Regulation Subchapter B—Relocation Allowances, Part 302-3—Relocation by Specific Type (www.gsa.gov).

Table B: Assigned to First Official Station outside the Continental United States (OCONUS)

Column 1— Relocation allowances that agency must pay or reimburse	**Column 2— Relocation allowances that agency has discretionary authority to pay or reimburse**
(1) Transportation of employee & immediate family member(s) (Part 302-4 of this chapter).	(1) Shipment of privately owned vehicle (POV) (Part 302-9 of this chapter).
(2) Per diem employee only (Part 302-4).	(2) Temporary quarters subsistence expense (TQSE) is not authorized in a foreign area, however, you may be entitled to the following under the Department of State Standardized Regulations (Government Civilians-Foreign Areas) which is available from the Superintendent of Documents, Washington, DC 20402. (a) Foreign Transfer Allowance (FTA) (Subsistence Expense) for quarters occupied temporarily before departure from the 50 states or the District of Columbia for a official station in a foreign area incident to a permanent change of station and travel to first official station overseas. (b) Temporary quarters subsistence allowance (TQSA) when a transfer is authorized to a foreign area. (c) The miscellaneous expense portion of the FTA is authorized incident to first official station travel to a foreign area.

(3) Transportation & temporary storage of household goods (Part 302-7 of this chapter).	(3) Use of relocation service companies only when transfer is to Alaska or Hawaii (Part 302-12 of this chapter).
(4) Extended storage of household goods (Part 302-8 of this chapter).	(4) Home marketing incentives only when transfer is to a non-foreign OCONUS area (Part 302-15 of this chapter).

Transferred Employees

Table A: Transfer between Official Stations in the Continental United States (CONUS)

Column 1— Relocation allowances that agency must pay or reimburse	Column 2— Relocation allowances that agency has discretionary authority to pay or reimburse
(1) Transportation & per diem for employee & immediate family member(s) (Part 302-4 of this chapter).	(1) Househunting per diem & transportation, employee & spouse only (Part 302-5 of this chapter).
(2) Miscellaneous moving expense (Part 302-16 of this chapter).	(2) Temporary quarters subsistence expense (TQSE) (Part 302-6 of this chapter).
(3) Sell or buy residence transactions or lease termination expenses (Part 302-11 of this chapter).	(3) Shipment of privately owned vehicle (POV) (Subpart B of Part 302-9 of this chapter).
(4) Transportation & temporary storage of household goods (Part 302-7 of this chapter).	(4) Use of a relocation services company.
(5) Extended storage of household goods (Part 302-8 of this chapter).[1]	(5) Property management services (Part 302-15 of this chapter).

(6) Transportation of a mobile home or boat used as a primary residence in lieu of the transportation of household goods (Part 302-10 of this chapter).	(6) Home marketing incentives (Part 302-14 of this chapter).
(7) Relocation income tax allowance (RITA) (Part 302-17 of this chapter).	

[1]**Note to Column 1, Item 5:** Only when assigned to a designated isolated official station in CONUS.

Table B: Transfer from CONUS to an Official Station outside the Continental United States (OCONUS)

Column 1— Relocation allowances that agency must pay or reimburse	Column 2— Relocation allowances that agency has discretionary authority to pay or reimburse
(1) Transportation & per diem for employee & immediate family member(s) (Part 302-4 of this chapter).	(1) Temporary quarters subsistence expense (TQSE) is not authorized in a foreign area, however, you may be entitled to the following under the Department of State Standardized Regulations (DSSR) (Government Civilians-Foreign Areas): (a) A Foreign Transfer Allowance (FTA) for quarters occupied temporarily before departure from the 50 states or the District of Columbia for a official station in a foreign area incident to a permanent change of station and travel to first official station overseas. (b) Temporary quarters subsistence allowance (TQSA).

(2) Miscellaneous expense allowance (Part 302-16 of this chapter).	(2) Property management services (Part 302-15 of this chapter).
(3) Transportation & temporary storage of household goods (Part 302-7 of this chapter).	(3) Shipment of a privately owned vehicle (Part 302-9 of this chapter).
(4) Extended storage of household goods (Part 302-8 of this chapter).	(4) Use of relocation service companies when transfer is to Alaska or Hawaii (Part 302-12 of this chapter).
(5) Relocation income tax allowance (RITA) (Part 302-17 of this chapter).[1]	(5) Home marketing incentives when transfer is to Alaska or Hawaii (Part 302-15 of this chapter).

[1]**Note to Column 1, Item 5:** Allowed when old and new official stations are located in the United States. Also allowed when instead of being returned to the former non-foreign area official station, an employee is transferred in the interest of the Government to a different non-foreign area official station from the official station from which transferred when assigned to the foreign official station.

Table C: Transfer from OCONUS Official Station to an Official Station in CONUS

Column 1— Relocation allowances that agency must pay or reimburse	Column 2— Relocation allowances that agency has discretionary authority to pay or reimburse
(1) Transportation & per diem for employee & immediate family member(s) (Part 302-4 of this chapter).	(1) Shipment of a privately owned vehicle (Part 302-9 of this chapter).
(2) Temporary quarters subsistence expense (TQSE) (Part 302-6 of this chapter).[1]	
(3) Miscellaneous expense allowance (Part 302-16 of this chapter).	

(4) Sell & buy residence transaction expenses or lease termination expenses (Part 302-11 of this chapter).[2]	
(5) Transportation & temporary storage of household goods (Part 302-7 of this chapter).	
(6) Extended storage of household goods only when assigned to a designated isolated official station in CONUS (Part 302-8 of this chapter).	
(7) Relocation income tax allowance (RITA) (Part 302-17 of this chapter).	

[1]**Note to Column 1, Item 2:** A TQSA under the DSSR may be authorized preceding final departure subsequent to the necessary vacating of residence quarters.
[2]**Note to Column 1, Item 4:** Allowed when old and new official stations are located in the United States. Also allowed when instead of being returned to the former non-foreign area official station, an employee is transferred in the interest of the Government to a different non-foreign area official station from the official station from which transferred when assigned to the foreign official station.

Table D: Transfer between OCONUS Official Stations

Column 1— Relocation allowances that agency must pay or reimburse	Column 2— Relocation allowances that agency has discretionary authority to pay or reimburse
(1) Transportation & per diem for employee & immediate family member(s) (Part 302-4 of this chapter).	(1) Shipment of a privately owned vehicle (POV) (Part 302-9 of this chapter).
(2) Temporary quarters subsistence expense (TQSE) (Part 302-6 of this chapter).[1]	(2) Property management services (Part 302-15 of this chapter).
(3) Transportation & temporary storage of household goods (Part 302-7 of this chapter).	

(4) Miscellaneous expense allowance (Part 302-16 of this chapter).	
(5) Extended storage of household goods (Part 302-8 of this chapter).	
(6) Relocation income tax allowance (RITA (Part 302-17 of this chapter).	

[1]**Note to Column 1, Item 2:** TQSA may be authorized under the DSSR.

Table E: Tour Renewal Agreement Travel

Column 1— Relocation allowances that agency must pay or reimburse	Column 2— Relocation allowances that agency has discretionary authority to pay or reimburse
(1) Transportation for employee & immediate family member(s) (Part 302-4 of this chapter).	
(2) Per diem for employee only (Part 302-4 of this chapter).	

Table F: Return from OCONUS Official Station to Place of Actual Residence for Separation

Column 1— Relocation allowances that agency must pay or reimburse	Column 2— Relocation allowances that agency has discretionary authority to pay or reimburse
(1) Transportation for employee & immediate family member(s) (Part 302-4 of this chapter).	(1) Shipment of a privately owned vehicle (POV) (Part 302-9 of this chapter).

(2) Per diem for employee only (Part 302-4 of this chapter).	
(3) Transportation & temporary storage of household goods (Part 302-7 of this chapter).	

Table G: Last Move Home for SES Career Appointees upon Separation

Column 1— Relocation allowances that agency must pay or reimburse	**Column 2— Relocation allowances that agency has discretionary authority to pay or reimburse**
(1) Transportation for employee & immediate family member(s) (Part 302-4 of this chapter).	(1) Shipment of privately owned vehicle (POV) (Subpart B of Part 302-9 of this chapter).
(2) Per diem for employee only (Part 302-4 of this chapter).	
(3) Transportation & temporary storage of household goods (Part 302-7 of this chapter).	
(4) Transportation of a mobile home or boat used as a primary residence in lieu of the transportation of household goods (Part 302-10 of this chapter).	

Table H: Temporary Change of Station (TCS)

Column 1— Relocation allowances that agency must pay or reimburse	Column 2— Relocation allowances that agency has discretionary authority to pay or reimburse
(1) Transportation & per diem for employee & immediate family member(s) (Part 302-4 of this chapter).	(1) Househunting trip expenses (Part 302-5 of this chapter).
(2) Miscellaneous expense allowance (Part 302-16 of this chapter).	(2) Temporary quarters subsistence expense (TQSE) (Part 302-6 of this chapter).
(3) Transportation & temporary or extended storage of household goods (Parts 302-7 and 302-8 of this chapter).	(3) Storage of one privately owned vehicle (POV) when assigned in support of a contingency operation as defined in 10 U.S.C. 1482a (c)(2) (Part 302-9 of this chapter).
(4) Transportation of a mobile home or boat used as a primary residence in lieu of the transportation of household goods (Part 302-10 of this chapter).	(4) Property management services (Part 302-15 of this chapter).
(5) Transportation of a privately owned vehicle (POV) Part 302-9 of this chapter).	
(6) Relocation income tax allowance (RITA) (Part 302-17 of this chapter).	

Table I: Assignment under the Government Employees Training Act (5 U.S.C. 4109)[1]

(1) Transportation of employee & immediate family member(s) (Part 302-4 of this chapter).
(2) Per Diem for employee (Part 302-4 of this chapter).
(3) Movement of household goods & temporary storage (Part 302-7 of this chapter).

[1]**Note to Table I:** The allowances listed in Table I may be authorized in lieu of per diem or actual expense allowances. This is not considered a permanent change of station.

Acronyms

A/OPC – agency/organization program coordinator

ATM – automated teller machine

CBA – centrally billed account

CBCA – Civilian Board of Contract Appeals

CFR – Code of Federal Regulations

CG – Comptroller General

CONUS – continental United States

CPP – City Pair Program

CTO – commercial/contract travel/ticket office

DoD – Department of Defense

DSSR – Department of State Standardized Regulations

DTMO – Defense Travel Management Office

EO – executive order

ETS – E-Gov Travel Service

FAR – Federal Acquisition Regulation

FTR – Federal Travel Regulation

GAO – Government Accountability Office

GARS – government administrative rate supplement

GOA – government automobile

GOV – government-owned vehicle

GSA – General Services Administration

GSBCA – General Services Board of Contract Appeals
GTR – government transportation request
HHG – household goods
HR – human resources
IBA – individually billed account
IG – inspector general
JFTR – Joint Federal Travel Regulations
JTR – Joint Travel Regulations
M&IE – meals and incidental expenses
OCCM – Office of Charge Card Management
OCONUS – outside the continental United States
OIG – Office of Inspector General
OMB – Office of Management and Budget
OPM – Office of Personnel Management
PCS – permanent change of station
PDS – permanent duty station
POV – privately owned vehicle
RIF – reduction in force
RRC – relocation resource center
SES – Senior Executive Service
TCS – temporary change of station
TDY – temporary duty
TMC – travel management center
TMS – Travel Management Service
TQSA – temporary quarters subsistence allowance
TQSE – temporary quarters subsistence expense
TTRA – Travel and Transportation Reform Act
U.S.C. – United States Code

Index

P

R

The Appropriations Law Answer Book: A Q & A Guide To Fiscal Law

William G. Arnold, CDFM-A

Now, there is an easy-to-use, straightforward guide to help everyone involved with appropriated funds. **The Appropriations Law Answer Book: A Q&A Guide to Fiscal Law** is the "go-to" resource for answers to fiscal law questions that arise in the federal workplace. This book condenses the content of the 2,000+ page Government Accountability Office's *Principles of Federal Appropriations Law* (the "Redbook"), providing a pertinent and usable resource for everyone who has responsibility for federal funds.

ISBN 978-1-56726-362-6 ■ Product Code B626 ■ 258 pages

Quick Reference to Federal Appropriations Law, Second Edition

John E. Jensen

Now in its second edition, *Quick Reference to Federal Appropriations Law, Second Edition* makes federal spending decisions even easier! No longer will you need to sort through thousands of pages to find the answers you need — this valuable reference explains the core appropriations laws in a condensed and accessible format with pertinent updates.

ISBN 978-1-56726-176-9 ■ Product Code B760 ■ 269 pages

Antideficiency Act Answer Book

William G. Arnold, CDFM-A, CCA

Antideficiency Act (ADA) violations within both the financial and audit communities are now at an all-time high. Violations often result from a lack of knowledge about what is — and what is not — permissible under the law. *The Antideficiency Act Answer Book* is an easy-to-understand question-and-answer tool that guides you through all the rules associated with the Antideficiency Act and helps you detect and report violations in a timely manner.

ISBN 978-1-56726-244-5 ■ Product Code B445 ■ 235 pages

Prompt Payment Act Answer Book

William G. Arnold, CDFM-A, CCA

It can be challenging for federal agencies to comply with the Prompt Payment Act. Although the basic rules are simple, they can be difficult to interpret and apply properly — until now. Designed as a reference, *The Prompt Payment Act Answer Book* lays out the prompt payment rules in a question-and-answer format, enabling readers to find answers to hundreds of specific questions. Practitioners will find the information they need to get and stay in compliance with the Prompt Payment Act and will benefit from real-world examples they can apply in everyday operations.

ISBN 978-1-56726-243-8 ■ Product Code B438 ■ 172 pages

Order today for a 30-day risk-free trial!

Visit **www.managementconcepts.com/pubs** or call **703-790-9595**